A Braided Cord

JIM WARREN

Patrick. Best wishes.

Jim

ISBN

978-1-4602-3348-1 (Hardcover)

978-1-4602-3349-8 (Paperback)

978-1-4602-3350-4 (eBook)

Produced by:

FriesenPress

Suite 300 – 852 Fort Street

Victoria, BC, Canada V8W 1H8

www.friesenpress.com

Distributed to the trade by The Ingram Book Company

Table of Contents

Without numbers are the world's wonders,
but none more wonderful than man.

Sophocles 496 to 406 BC

Acknowledgements

COVER The photo is a simple grouping of three old books, unidentified and piled on one another in random fashion with the braided cord of sisal coiled in some way beside or partly on top of them with one end uncoiled and prominent so as to clearly demonstrate the three strands. The focus should be on the cord. A single lit candle that has the appearance of having mostly burned down with wax drippings prominent. Whether a single old hand should be included I can't say! I need flesh in the midst. The grouping is bathed in a pool of light surrounded by blackness and placed on a worn table top. It can suggest, time, diversity, age, enlightenment, effort and flesh. The cord may seem animated. The hand that grasps the cord absorbs its power.

Thanks to Janet Dwyer, Salt Spring Photographer for this cover photograph that so clearly illustrated my idea for the theme of this book. Thanks to my friend John Mills who was, and still is, teaching me to read.

The book is an extension of the book An Elderly Eclectic Gentleman, written earlier, and published by Friesen Press, and is derived from the blog of the same name, elderlyeclecticgentleman.blogspot.com.

PHILOSOPHY

Crumbs

Write your own moral stand
And designate it as the high road
Cut away from those who don't walk it
Enjoy the heady view
Your standpoint allows it and your ramparts seem secure

And

You are worthy to gather the crumbs
You are worthy to eat the whole loaf

But

Your concrete doesn't bind
The stones loosen and roll
It's a long way to fall
All is vanity

The Palimpsest

When my career was young and I knew what I knew, I found myself suddenly surrounded by an exceedingly dense fog. I could not find my way and I was directionless. I reached with all my strength into the dense fog, well up to my shoulder and suddenly something touched my hand. I could feel it move away, but I grasped it in desperation so it wouldn't escape. I pulled it out of the mist. It was a parchment. It appeared old: brown, wrinkled, lined with age. On its surface there was a script, written line by line, filling the parchment face, full of strange cryptic characters. When the fog lifted I sat at my desk and tried to imagine what I had been given. I did not understand the script and so I concluded that those writings therefore must be irrelevant. As a result, I took my eraser and erased the printed characters. Having done so, there were still the indents on the parchment face where the earlier writer had pressed on the stylus. On that blank page, now available to me, I wrote a treatise on the nature of modern medicine. I had suddenly seemed to find my way; I wasn't directionless, and I knew what I knew. Still, I was haunted by the strange characters I had erased and became aware that I knew what I didn't know. Later, I had a dream in which the written description of that exquisite simulacrum from the past appeared to me in translation. I realized that I had erased and overwritten that former script because of the hubris I felt about the present and the failure to know the relevance of what I never knew. I erased my treatise on modern medicine and burnished, with my forebears' ashes, the indented parchment to bring the old indentations back into life. A palimpsest made through the fog and mist of time was a gift to teach me what I needed to know.

A Braided Cord

With a braided hawser-laid cord of three strands that are wound together with one another, each strand provides its share of strength to the triadic nature of the cord. When the cord is weighted, the braiding as a whole imparts elasticity and it lengthens because of the torque moment the loaded braid creates. This is at no cost to the strength of the cord. After the braided cord is stretched, there arises an equal and opposite force from the braid to whatever weight it must endure. The strand of Reason weaves through and around the strands of Flesh and Passion. The strand of Ego weaves through and around the strands of Id and Super-Ego. The strand of Reason weaves through and around the strands of Tradition and Scripture. The strand of Reason weaves through and around the strands of Body and Soul. Where the first fibers that made up a strand arose from is a mystery, but they are called Spirit. Which strand was constructed last from these fibers, we may surmise from history, but each strand is made of the same spun fibers of Spirit. The whole is more than the sum of its parts because of the integral moment provided by the braid design. What is certain is that aside from which strand was built last (possibly Reason) when weighted down, the three-strand cord becomes longer and stronger with the strands working together, acting as one. The hand that grasps the cord absorbs its power.

Revision

Years ago, I was a member of a college council. Our CEO had a painting by Jack Shadbolt hung in his office. A fellow doctor had donated it to the college. The painter sometimes retrieved paintings he was not entirely pleased with from their owners, and repainted the parts he didn't like! The painting of ours that I recall was of the old wooden Marpole footbridge in Olympic City. The artist had painted people standing on the bridge, looking down at the water of the Fraser Arm. He repainted the foreground and returned the revised work. It would be tough to collect all the books one sold to change the lines that, in retrospect, offended oneself. Certainly if you own the copyright and haven't sold it you can republish your book without the dirty or underwhelming bits, but that doesn't change what is already out there. It's tough to alter the past in your life where the lines were troubling. You just have to forgive yourself and crank up every morning with the new knowledge and the new humility you may be blessed with. Then one can republish oneself with the current received wisdom where, again, you still own the copyright. Never sell it! Once you have republished yourself, you can go and make a whole new set of mistakes. Unlike the occasional painting, there is no pigment opaque enough to cover up the original me. I guess editing oneself is a lifelong process, but if you don't publish sometime, then you aren't here. Shit happens, but humble pie always has enough calories to help one grow bigger!

The Retrospectroscope

An endoscopy is a procedure that allows one to look within the body with a fiberoptic tool called an endoscope. Scope means to look at things, or, alternatively, the extent of things. Retrospect is seeing the past anew. To look within oneself, if you like, we will call the procedure a psychoscopy, and to that end, the retrospectroscope will be advanced slowly and deliberately along the human lumen, viewing it thoughtfully through the lens of the scope. It will display the interior of the personal channel we have created over the years. The channel isn't called a "lumen" for nothing, though it may be dark until illuminated! The tool isn't called "scope" for nothing—call it, "to see the space in real time." To see clearly, the lens of the flexible scope must not be fogged up or scratched and the light source for illumination must be bright. The lesions of the past will appear clearly through the scope, in bold relief, if the light is right and the lens not opaque. What you see is not always what you want to see. If you seek to find your anima one's posture is difficult to master and sometimes painful, but self-examination is usually worth it. There are no biopsy forceps with psychoscopy, so one cannot excise the lesions one discovers; we must merely observe and learn as the diagnostician would. Like all endoscopic procedures, regular psychoscopy assessments are of value insofar as they provide self-knowledge, even if eradicating the past lesions is not possible. One cannot change the past, but one may redress the past! One can record one's findings and describe the intricacies of the pathology for others. The modern endoscopes have cameras and video screening that allows ease of homework. You can reacquaint yourself with causality and preventative actions and provide wisdom for others who are without your years of experience or who lack the inclination necessary for acquiring such a tool or taking such action. The good physician may give advice, but it may fall on deaf ears. So too it was once with me! The lesions we produce in life, and the blocks over which we stumble are also the whetstones for what we become. I always learned more from my stumbles than from my successes. To know the interior man, and find the other self, we scope with good illumination and fortitude!

Ruminants

Yesterday, when I looked out the window on Lotus Island, I said to the pianist, "Look, there is a doe and a yearling lying on our footpath, chewing their cud!" Their front legs were crossed in complete repose; a posture not adapted to rapid takeoff. They stayed on the path for a good part of the afternoon. It's safe here! I guess in another place and time, they, and all the other Class Ruminantia, for that matter, were often surrounded by predators. Mother Nature demanded rapid food gathering in sites of danger by her ruminants. They had to always be alert and ready to flee, and only later would they have a chance to regurgitate and break down the snatched food at leisure, in found safety and sanctuary. I ask myself from time to time, why I would write about trivial matters such as two deer relaxing in a sanctuary of sorts when the world is going through such monumental events: war, revolution, economic fears, shaken faith, individuals on the cusp of disaster. And here I am today, ruminating along with my deer. Chewing snatched cud of information and ideas, pulled rapidly from the trees of knowledge, gathered in a hurry, and not fully digested! Much of that information was gathered during the momentum of a hurried life, in which one was feeding quickly. I guess, to answer my own question," I am writing for myself in part, and it is not trivial!" I should really call it "reflection" since the psychiatrists unfortunately have now tainted "rumination." It's nothing more than having a good chew at material that you bring up, in order to break it down again. In a sea of troubles, we have to reach for a plank to stop ourselves from drowning. We have to float! I guess my plank in life is to celebrate the ordinary stuff of existence that may give some buoyancy. Age gives one time to ruminate/reflect on the information gathered in a hurry. Now I can repose with my legs crossed and let go!

Fundamentals of Life

Ingestion, procreation and evacuation are the fundamentals of life. Everything else is ancillary—devoted to serving these fundamentals. If one wishes to discuss life, one will miss its essence if one sticks to the ancillary and the ornamental. To fail to embrace the fundamentals first, is to overlook the humanness of one's vessel. Those of us in the practice of surgery, anatomy, or physiology are, by necessity, engaged with the human vessel and in constant contact with its fundamentals. Whether a Paramoecium (a one-celled tube) or a Homo sapiens (the complex multi-cellular collection of bundled tubing of which we consist), we ingest, evacuate and reproduce. When you spend your day with a finger in the tubes of the bowel, gallbladder, or pharynx, pinching and fingering the ancillary sidekick, the ureter, the common bile duct, or the soft palate, all of which are conduits that are traveled daily, you have an intimate understanding of a fundamental human essence. If your finger is in the aorta or the portal vein, or the carotid artery or left ventricle, tubes which serve and support the fundamentals, you understand how the system works. The brain is the largest sex organ and the greatest forager, orchestrating the tubes. You will know that if the fundamentals suddenly are not in working order, the brain crashes to emergency mode, concentration on other matters is impossible, and the tubing becomes the most important thing in the world! Great art, music, philosophy, love, compassion, indwelling spirit, science of particles, universe and earth: all of these are evolved from this bundle of tubes we call our vessel, and though normally worshiped, are temporarily set aside. It is easy to forget that without the fundamentals we are nothing! This is not understood by a Paramoecium, who has not been gifted with abstract thinking, but is a hard fact to remember for a smart Homo sapiens. "You know," said my other and better self, when he looked at this foregoing screed, "you are being a bit coarse and your fleshly strand in the braided cord is running on its own. Your surgical gestalt is puffed up today. Is it that you need a little more attention from me because we're all a bit tired of how you favour the flesh over spirit and intellect in the cord of life? Without something to worship there is no life!"

Evil

In our weekly literature group we are working through some of Edmund Spenser's The Faerie Queene. In Book One, the evil arch-magician, Archimago, is a strong presence in the narrative. As we discussed a Canto of Book One, I mentioned as an aside the inherent evil of Ariel Castro, a topical current event I thought mildly relevant to our discussion. I was immediately challenged by my friend Dennis, who said, "You think you are superior to Castro!" I was taken aback, but, defensive, I quickly replied, "Well, I don't think I would secrete away three little girls and abuse them for ten years with ropes and chains."— "Maybe not", he said, "But you are talking about the law, not nature, because none of us is different. We are all of the same substance and have a universal dark side! It's just that some of us don't recognize it!" I don't want to put words in Dennis' mouth, but it was a week ago and the words of his are roughly as I have related. I have since thought about it and he is right about me. I was too glib and in the right circumstance I believe I, and many others, are capable of almost anything that would seem evil in retrospect. My defense to Dennis was that people must be accountable for their actions. He agreed with that, but clearly separated justice and morality. I guess the question I ask is: is there a moral man? Is there an honest man? Do we have the courage to face our dark side? Do we fall back on the idea that the devil influenced our evil actions? I have to assent; we are all made of the same clay. In the movie Lawrence of Arabia, the moment of realization that seized Lawrence with grief, when he suddenly broke down, was when he said he had shot a man with his gun. The horror of his action however, occurred when he confessed, not that he killed the man, but that he enjoyed the killing. The insights we gain in the book club, spun from the magic of Spenser, are far more than the narrative itself. It comes also from the clean and honest exchanges that arise from the seed. Literature of this nature must be read as a group to fully harvest this fruit!

Homeostasis

Even though the hurricane season has passed by, I have been thinking somewhat idly about life existing in the eye of the storm. Homeostasis! Perfect equilibrium for a little while! If you think about meeting Abraham Maslow's Pyramid of Needs, I believe the eye of the cyclone remains the perfect sanctuary; still, it would be a job to stay in it and not drift sideways into the vortex. I'm not sure that marshaling the effort needed to stay in the calm eye of the storm is what life is all about! Take your pills, seek friends and love, have a good job, get insurance, be good, have confidence, create a beautiful home and children, join a good book club, join the service club, grow old gently, die in your sleep! There has to be more than this. Maslow had the idea that all these met needs would ease the development of self-actualization! Seems to me that it is outside the eye of the storm where self-actualization happens. Homeostasis by definition is stasis; Homo sapiens standing still on the airport belt, carried along in a measured pace. Wow! Unfortunately, we need stress to temper our calm. Cold water drench after the fire! If you don't know black, you will never fully appreciate white. If you haven't been buffeted by the winds of ill fortune you will never know the quality of your fortitude! Better that you have an illness, lose a job, lose a love, get kicked out of a club and recover from these to know you are made for the vortex as well as the eye of the cyclone. Leonard, in his song, 'Famous Blue Raincoat,' says, "Are you living for nothing now?"—"No," I say, "I'm taking a chance!"

Come see, come saw

The best definition of "been there, done that" is "come see, come saw!" A cursory look at Google does not come up with this definition, which is too bad—but so what! By that definition, everything is said to be old hat. Such a person has become fatigued by the ordinariness of the succession of events that pass by daily. That individual is not easily entertained. That individual is not easily inspired. It is difficult to enthuse or even interest those who know a bit of everything and think they have seen all there is to see. The thrust of my blog and my book, Elderly Eclectic Gentleman, was that the ordinary is truly extraordinary. That was my whole point. Some have said that the book is interesting and that it has resonated with some of my readers so far, but I was told it couldn't be marketed effectively because the subjects are too ordinary and the writing too personal! I haven't succeeded in making the point. "For instance," says one, "why would any one care about your piece on 'Puberty, Jim has hair'?"—Well, I have thought about that assertion. The appearance of that first tuft of black, in that place! Why would anyone not care about that? It is a seminal event in everyone's life, figuratively or literally! Death of childhood! An enthused but fearsome step into the unknown! It was more important than anything else to the adolescent. Welcomed or feared, it was so important we can remember the date it occurred, and the place we first observed it. Personal? Not really; universal in fact! It is an example, par excellence, of the ordinary being extraordinary. If it does not resonate with you, it is because you have forgotten what matters. I cannot help you. I can only tell you! Do not be life-weary. Don't be come see, come saw!

Mankind as Meat

A former rector of mine, with whom I had a friendly, but occasionally check-ered relationship, was mildly intrigued, and possibly repulsed, that my job as an orthopedic surgeon involved cutting into the human body. He often greeted me with the salutation, "How is Chop-Chop today?" It was never a question, though he may have believed it was. I think he thought this greeting was funny. I was never quite able to cope with this somewhat rhetorical question satisfactorily. I brushed it off as his unique sense of humour and shrugged with a smile. It is, however, a classical example of words that betray thoughts. It did provide me with some insight into the philosophic gestalt of some, that since we are made in the image of God, it is not important to embrace the fact that we are meat. We are meat, and God and Nature; all his handiwork is one, and much of his handiwork is meat. Luckily for me, my son, also a rector, was with me one day when I was greeted by my friend the rector, who said gaily to me in his usual fashion, "Have you done any chop-chop today?" At least a verb this time rather than a noun. It was a marginal semblance of probity; better to chop-chop rather than be Chop-Chop. My boy looked him over and asked in response, "Have you done any mumble-mumble today?" Done rather than are; Reverent Mumble-Mumble! It's a blessing to have someone stand up for you. My rector's wife, who was party to this exchange, mused about Chop-Chop. "Maybe what he asks is rude," she thought aloud. I think not! It is all a matter of perspective. "I worship, therefore I am," we say. "I think, therefore I am," we say. "I cut meat; I screw bones together, therefore I am!" I said. Thinking further, maybe he stumbled into the truth inadvertently. We are both the noun and the verb. In part, we are what we do!

Heart vs Brain

Soul vs Sense; Architecture vs Horticulture; Man vs Woman. How the pianist has put up with my plant peccadilloes over the years is a tribute to her tolerance of my relative inanity! Since I am a known pruneophobic, I have so far succeeded in withstanding all efforts to curb both my enthusiasm for large house plants, and for allowing them to grow wherever they choose to wander. I am not a stern parent with plants as I want them to be happy and free as I am. We share the same molecules. They are like my brothers. My 30-year-old rubber tree (Fiscus elastica) is about 25 feet tall and the stairs to our bedroom are now hidden from view in its underbrush. The female realtor suggested, careful not to cause offense, that the architecture of the stairway was of such interest it would be an advantage to see it. My equally old Hoya vine climbs up to the top of a 28-foot beam and balances the rubber tree. The realtor cautiously and cleverly suggested that a mighty beam of that nature might usefully be seen advantageously as well, rather than assumed to be there! These two plants harmonize together; the hoya beam opposite the hypotenuse of the rubber tree. No one but me can hear their point and counterpoint. A second Hoya in the dining room had penetrated into the ceiling tongue and groove boards in an attempt to escape the room through the roof. No one but me seems to understand their need for freedom. This Easter weekend will be a watershed for these plants since the pianist, my daughters and the realtor have all agreed that I have now reached the end of the road and must control both my neurosis and my plants. They were kind and no one suggested I was overly weird. Radical pruning of the rubber tree will produce tears of white sap from the tree, so tissues are a must for us both! The Hoyas will cling to ceiling and beam, and we may hear them scream when pruned, so earplugs are also a must. Since I am an Asclepiad by profession, I am related in a sense to the hoya (Asclepiadaceae), my cousin, by name as well as by the molecules we hold in common. I know that the women are right! Group intervention was necessary! Group therapy may be needed for plants of our nature, but architecture and common sense has prevailed. Harmony between house and plants, harmony between me and the pianist, harmony between sense and sensibility will prevail. Still, I hope romance is not entirely dead.

Products of Conception

When I was the Chief of the Medical Staff at Lotus City hospital in the olden days (1983,1984, I think) we had an abortion committee. This committee was a "sage" collection of physicians who volunteered to assess cases that fitted what then constituted the law, which required medical input on the written request by the patient's doctor that we provide an abortion. Abortions were performed on the basis of the stated fact that the pregnancy was a threat to the life or the health of the mother. Now, to put it in perspective, the committee was composed of a selection of pro-life and pro-choice inclined doctors all of whom volunteered, and it varied in composition from week to week, but the committee mix selected was always chosen by the hospital secretary to the administrator. Curiously, there was always a preponderance of pro-choice members each week. I said to Ms F. the then secretary one day, "Why don't you pick the names of the doctors out of a hat?" "Yes," she said, "that's a good idea." Of course, the composition ratios never changed, but I set aside my ambiguity in the role. I am not proud of myself for evading issues of such deep and divisive nature, but I'm only human, and despite my role, I was operating under denial because it was too tough otherwise and I had a hundred other hospital issues. From time to time, in the days of spontaneous abortion, if you held and watched a perfect 15 week old foetus in a kidney basin as it made silent mouth-opening signs, chest fluttering, and limb-writhing activity, it seemed like a person. Thereupon, you might be forgiven for having strong feelings develop about the nature of personhood. In the 60s, the Sisters of St. Anne in the other hospital in Lotus City used to baptize the foetuses in the operating room. On the other hand, if you were the parent of a 13-year-old girl who ran away from home because she was pregnant by her brother and you were in agony to find her before she did something desperate to herself, you also might also have strong feelings about the nature of personhood. These examples, of course, occupy either end of the pole. Maybe Jeremiah 1:5 is wrong. No amount of abstract reasoning by elderly judges, inconstant politicians, scriptural literalists or fossilized medievalists will answer this question. What is certain is that the debate of, "what is a person?" is a new pathway to the abortion question. There may be an answer, but there is no solution arising that satisfies! Up to now, pragmatism rules. The adoption of the term, "products of conception," is a cold and clinical description; it is an escape clause that depersonalizes what, if not a person, seems at least to be a life or close to it, and "a product" appears more a market concept than a thinking person's image. Maybe it always has. Sad! Shall we content ourselves therefore that we are merely the same as any tissue. Products of conception meet that test of comfort. I have no solutions that are hopeful other than that, if possible, we should see ourselves as more than just tissue. Alternatively, it may be more convenient to avoid the argument by just seeing ourselves as tissue, at any age, that talks rather than barks! Hard Words.

Happenstance

If you know that some of the seemingly trivial events in your life led to consequences that happened without your control, you may have some concern about the uncertainty of life and your prospects. If you believe that life in the final analysis occurs without much control, like Brownian Movement, and that flecks of dust particles, or all particles for that matter, just collide, or don't, and that control is ultimately of limited value anyway, then "que sera, what ever will be, will be." Then, it just ain't yer fault! If, however, you consider happenstance, that is, that there are directions, as yet unknown, to the seemingly unrelated or sometime trivial events leading to whatever end you may arrive at, one will therefore have a somewhat fatalistic point of view. I have no doubt all of these preconditions are operative in life, and I can't help but think that there were some coincidences in my life that were directed by something other than myself. Things beyond my control, things that are not always randomized, but a predestined linkage that led to a chain of events that were arranged from beyond. Does it not feel good that there may be some guidance in this life? — "Oh James my boy," says the skeptic, "You have a remarkable ability to kid yourself." I still say, does it not feel good that there could be some outside force that will connect whatever dots there are to connect? I find it comforting to think that the direction is not all up to me and that I cannot always hold my destiny in my hand and direct it to do the right thing, or know the right thing for that matter. That I am not powerful enough to avoid all the pitfalls in life, or alternatively the pitfalls in my life may be for my own good. If the Brownian Movement is in an epic battle in life with endogenous Control or exogenous Happenstance for our lives, it's never winner take all, but we had best be on our knees that it is not just Brownian randomness. I'm cheering for Control and directed Happenstance: being anal or hanging loose! I think a dose of both! Not either/or! Or very probably all three!

Just Who Do You Think You Are?

As I lay in bed asleep last night I woke up with a start and a small inner voice said, "Just who do you think you are? What right have you to keep saying "you" in your writing, or your diatribes in fact, as if you are lecturing to some invisible novitiate who is hanging onto your every pathetic idea. Take your last blog, Happenstance; all I can say is what a pedantic piece of nonsense masquerading as something deep. Drivel! Why don't you stick to the strange little episodes of your life events, some of which are exaggerated, but at least less pretentious than your meager ideas of life. And your putative book cover, that's another matter. You haven't even left enough rope to hang yourself."—Well, you can see I am having a crisis of confidence! I admit that from time to time I have over-rated my more puny ideas of life. "It isn't so bad that you write these ideas of life," said the small voice, "but that you think you are on the high road when in fact you are a poseur, because you keep preening yourself as you write, presuming that it is all newness." I suppose that I am grateful for the small voice even though down deep I admit it is not all that comforting. Still, if I believe that what comes along is for the good, whatever comes, I'll accept that Jobian concept, at least for the moment till the next bad thing comes along for me, as it will and then I'll chuck Job again. I'm human. Pontificating is unfortunately a fault of mine, but magnified as a fault if one has no business doing it! Maybe, as the pianist says, I should stop saying "you," as if I was entitled to teach some-buddy and use "one" instead, or better still "I" when it really is me, not you. Moreover, your inner voice may be on target for you more than mine is for me. Anyway, I have to ask the small inner voice, "Just who do you think you are, because I'm not sure? I'm not going to take everything you say as gospel." I may be kidding myself, but even if some of it strains the imagination, according to the voices, it is at least my attempt to be honest. There is a lot of imagination out there in the writing world so I am entitled to contribute mine as well, including Happenstance.

Walking

Somehow, I have probably driven the three short blocks from home to town a thousand times, while passing the features along the way. They are as familiar to me as the details of the interior of my house, or so I thought they were. I've said I could walk the distance in my sleep without foundering. Not so. I have been grounded for a while lately, so I have been unable to drive. I have been unwell and am beginning to rehabilitate by walking. Ambling is closer to the description of my ambulant adventures. It is closer in nature to the adventurous walking that a child in no hurry would do. What struck me with such intensity when I wandered along was the myriad things that I had missed in driving past one thousand times. My trail today was a zigzag beside the roadway and into the grassy byways. The trail was punctuated by stop and go, periods and dashes. I saw disuse and decay, new hope and splendor. I saw trial and error, failure and success. I encountered friends and strangers, talked to some and nodded to others. It's hard not to acknowledge passersby on the way to a small town. A fish store closed out of season; a stone sculptor's studio is empty since his death; a towering new apartment block is climbing a rock face; a rotting house is buried from view on a waterfront slope at the end of the harbor; a band shell is ready to make music; unused wharfage and rotting steps to the harbour are blocked off, and all the wild shrubs and trees and byways lie between them. I pass a marina with a few winter boats and signs forbidding parking other than for guests and staff, and a church open to all to park. That, of course, is the macro I looked at, but each feature, in fact, was a picture that invited one to stand there and see the micro in it all. I think I saw what a painter might see. I finally came to the town and the micro is familiar there, because after a drive, I have always, perforce, walked around in the town. That walking then becomes directed, purpose-driven and adult, and the muse takes a rest.

Justice and Fairness

Who gets to eat the most and why: is it just or fair and are they the same thing? With justice you get what you deserve. With fairness you deserve what they get. The pianist and I were sitting in the car at noon today having lunch at Beacon Hill Park. It was cold outside, so we ate in the car rather than on the park bench by the flowerbeds. The Mallards, man and wife, gaudy and plain, two striking seagulls and several funereal crows wandered around idly looking for a free meal. The crows are the first to identify the eaters in the car. When the pianist had her fill of sandwiches, she tore off the crusts to feed the ducks who were at first oblivious, but were now the closest, attracted to the car by the crows. The ducks, despite conjugality, began to vie with one another politely; just ramped up the waddle and began to eat their fill. The seagulls rushed over, but the safe distance they allow in proximity to humans is further than the ducks do, so they were nearly out of range from the spoils. Now, the pianist likes ducks better than seagulls, even if the gulls are more beautiful, but she is compelled to insist on fairness, called sharing, not rewarding! The result has her straining to meet the gulls' cries with her throwing arm. The gulls may be beautiful, but they are stupid, so when food looms, they sound off rather than shutting up, and when their colleagues arrived, they fought them for the food. It's hard to call it justice when the benefactor has to strain to give you what you need and you summon your friends and then battle for it with them. They have also learned to scream, "See me! See me!" At least it sounds like that! The pianist, in the interest of fairness and accommodation, took pity and hurled the crust portions to them as far as a crust would fly! I think this concern for equitable distribution is a female characteristic arising from the matronly urge to meet the needs of all: the long and the short and the tall. I think justice would give the gulls zilch! The cacophony from the seagulls drew more agitation from the crows, who arrived in force, but they have an even longer allowable safe distance to maintain from the human food source. It was impossible for her to meet their need. They looked forlorn as the pianist tried her best to break bread with them. They just couldn't outmuscle the gulls, couldn't cozy up to the humans like the ducks, and the pianist couldn't throw that far to moving targets. Crows are smarter than gulls and faster than ducks, but if they want justice, they are going to have work at it like everyone else, use their brains and take risks to finesse the big boys! Or else eat alone! Justice doesn't come without a price.

Original Ideas

Someone in our little group said today that he doubted there were any original ideas. We discussed that and concluded that it could be true but you would have to know everything that there is to know and everything that is going to be known in order to arrive at that opinion. If we go back to Ecclesiastes 1,9 we are told, "There is nothing new under the sun. What has been done will be done again." These were Bronze Age people of course, so they may be forgiven for confusing thinking and doing. They can also be forgiven for thinking there was no more to learn in their time. Some of us may well have to be forgiven for the same thing. We may just not recall what has been done or considered before, where we heard it, where it was recorded, where a small light was lit that we observed. If one thinks one has a lot of original thoughts, there is a chance one hasn't read much, or observed a lot, or has a short attention span! We are often just building blocks, piling onto the genius of others! Adding something more! Adding greatly more. It's a fine line. Those who create, as Isaac Newton said of himself, "Stand on the shoulders of giants." Ideas arise in some fashion, often as an unconscious acquisition of a resource discovered in the past to fulfill the then current job. The keyhole collection of information read, seen, heard, thought, is acquired where the creator innocently refashioned someone's material, looking at it from a different angle. Even the kernel of an idea or observation expressed elsewhere is fodder! If you think you are a clever fellow initiating new thoughts, remember that three pound organ in your skull is more than a concurrent data collector and electrical panel. It has its own life force that cannot be controlled and which reinvents itself again and again, taking in from the world more than we will ever know and providing us more than we will ever recognize. Three pounds of mystery whose ideas are its own and immeasurable, unknowable, connected to a greatness beyond our ken!

Turf the Old

I observed during my times visiting our son in Scotland that the Beech tree (Fagus sylvatica), does not shed its previous year's leaves until late in the spring despite the cold winter temperatures in Europe. The beech hedges, as seen widely distributed in Scotland, retain the browning and yellowed saw-toothed leaves throughout the winter, in contrast to almost all other leaves of deciduous trees, which conveniently and expeditiously retire to the turf in the fall in order to make way for the young leaf growth in the spring. The old Beech leaves are much more stubborn about going, and need the young growth in the spring to expand and force the old leaf attachment from its tenacious foothold. The elderly Beech leaves serve a minor purpose, I suppose, in that they winter over and thereby increase the winter density of the hedges that moderate the wind. However, the appearance of the winter hedge is reminiscent of elderly gentlemen whose role is come and gone, but who won't depart! Eventually, the youth will push them out and fulfill their role of a fresh leafy windbreak, as well as provide new life to the plant. Because the old are reluctant to leave, the mess to clean up after their departure detracts from the work to cultivate the new growth. If they only knew! Why don't these old leaves go quickly in the fall like all self-respecting oldsters and give new additional vitality to the compost over the winter, as well as space for the new buds? Providing good compost for the young is a duty of the old! I wonder if this question is horticultural or philosophical? They are the same! Aristotle says, "Nature does nothing in vain!" It is incumbent on us then, to consider that Aristotle may still be correct and therefore our need arises to seek to understand Nature's reasons. William of Ockham said, in effect, the correct answer is usually the simplest answer. If we believe that Mother Nature is always wise, then there must be a good reason that the Beech is true to its nature. It is tempting perhaps to say the leaves stay on to protect the cottage-dwellers from cold Scottish winds, parenting and sheltering as it were; but that is a benefit, not a reason. Even more likely; consider the willingness of the young buds to avoid dispossessing their old from the perch into the cold turf before their time, dried up and withered though they may be. Compassionate nurture at home by the young as it were. I like to think that Aristotle, Ockham and Mother Nature would be sympathetic to that point of view. Allowing the old to retire to new roles on their own terms! Thank God for sweet children and Orthopedic partners!

Re-creation

This is not sport! It's serious business! Listening to the current concern that mankind will falter with the expected looming changes in climate, food production, and population gives a new sense of urgency that we must alter the environment! When Jacob Bronoski wrote the screenplay for The Ascent of Man, his thesis was that mankind itself was capable of adaptating to changes and not a victim of the natural environment as were some other life forms. The capacity for abstract reasoning and foresight; the ability to change, adapt and thrive in all manner of adversity, was in the past, and still is, in its best measure, peculiar to man alone! We don't have to mutate in order to survive. Civilizations came and went, but mankind evolved in its capacity to adapt! The vulnerability of the less adaptable life forces that surround us will depend on the human capability to address the changes to come, in the interest of all. Currently, pessimism seems rampant! The media is full of dirt and gloom. The comment boards are dominated by the haters and polemicists. The Jeremiads are in full gallop down the hill. In our little group, we discussed this week the sins of the flesh we all possess. We spoke about how it was necessary for us to repress these desires in order to function in society. We took note of the selfish side of ourselves that sees the world as there for our immediate needs. What we didn't talk about was the nobility of mankind; the love, the drive, the intellect and the willingness of people to sacrifice to the greater good and to put off immediate gratification for the sake of a greater and later good. I brought it up in the group, but it went nowhere since we all prefer speaking of sin over goodness. Surely, there is a balance in mankind that has become obscured lately. If we are to survive and thrive in these seasons of change, then re-creation will need to occur with the opening, not closing, of the human spirit; we cannot hunker down, but must utilize the ever present noble side of our nature to open up and embrace the challenge of change with optimism. In the meantime, the downfall of some of us is procrastination. Capability is not a substitute for implementation.

MEDICINE

The Doctor's Dilemma

I was speaking with a friend about Downton Abbey and Lady Mary Crawley's dilemma with the Turkish gentleman who, given his age, must have had a fatal arrhythmia during intercourse. It reminded me of a similar, little known, but celebrated circumstance in Lotus City a bit after the mid 20th century when I began practice there. The city was very small at that time and medical practices were both tight and longitudinal, so the same physicians often attended families virtually from cradle to grave. As a result of this, patient and doctor loyalties were high. The doctor of whom I speak attended, for years, two carriage trade families who lived in the same neighborhood as him. One night he received a midnight call from his patient, the wife of a prominent businessman, in a panic, that a friend of her's had died in her bed. The man who died, a lawyer, was also the doctor's patient, a widower who had enjoyed a meal, and later, congress with the lady since her husband was away on business. Unfortunately, good living had rendered the older lawyer somewhat unfit for such action. Faced with such a situation and the possible eruption of a scandal involving two of his patient's families, the doctor's dilemma arose. The man had clearly had a heart attack at the time. As a result, the doctor and the lady, fueled no doubt by adrenaline, carried the man to the doctor's car and transported him to his house and put him in his own bed with new pajamas and tucked him in. The doctor then made a house call in the morning and called the coroner. The question of course is, what was the moral imperative that contended with the legal requirement of the doctor? A physician has a duty to the country, his colleagues and to his regulatory body to obey the law. He also owes a duty to the welfare of his patients at some cost, if necessary. He risked his medical practice by illegal transport of a human body from the place of sudden death in order to cover up the truth. However, dead is dead and a bed is a bed! What was the harm? It would have been easier for the doctor to avoid criticism by a self- righteous tack. He took a chance! In a small city where everyone knew everyone's business, or so they thought, the secret was kept for years. Succor for the innocent of the families I suppose, and avoiding the trials and near disasters that befell Lady Mary.

Masterly Inactivity

Voltaire once wrote, "The wise physician amuses his patient while nature affects the cure." That would have appealed to Hippocrates. We used to have a phrase for that intelligence of the physician to sometime stay the hand: Masterly Inactivity! It may have been first coined for Obstetrical Care, but by extension a small, but distinct segment of patients benefit from the need for this approach. This active pursuit of inactivity has nothing to do with interest or disinterest of the patient on the part of the physician. It simply means that when there is nothing to do, do nothing stupid; or that when there is nothing to do, do nothing, Stupid! Patients may be frequently unhappy with this approach, even those sufficiently sophisticated who have been counseled that diagnosis, continuing observation, and prognosis is all that is required for their condition! After some time taken at explanation of masterly inactivity and its indications, the response often still is, "For heaven's sake, you have to do something rather than nothing!" The simple fact is that many conditions are self-limiting and meddlesome interference is counterproductive; other conditions inevitably worsen; the clinical course unaffected, or complicated, by treatment! Hippocrates' aphorism applied for this state of being is also good advice for the wise physician, "Cure occasionally, comfort always!" He also wrote—"The role of the physician is refusal to treat those overpowered by these diseases with the knowledge that medical art is unavailing in these cases."—Of course, Hippocrates was in practice in 400 BC and there were not the tools we have today, nor were the expectations for cure so great then. Reputations for success are often cheaply achieved by the timing of active treatment for a self-limiting condition just before its denouement. Credit where none is due thereby is still useful, at least for the reputation of the practitioner until his next case falls apart. Useless treatments applied to conditions where deterioration is inevitable can always be excused with, "They tried everything and they worked so hard to help!" That specious remark may provide some comfort that there was never neglect for the lack of trying, but unless it was accompanied by reality, there is nothing so cruel as engendering false hope!

Setting Science aside, the Art of Medicine does not include taking credit for Mother Nature, and burdensome treatments for untreatable conditions. The line between Hope, Comfort, and Reality needs a careful tread! Somehow, the ideas of a French realist philosopher and a Greek physician can be still relevant today.

Communication

Ronald Reagan was said to be the Great Communicator! Style and Substance. Short and Sweet and Succinct. But hold it! We know he had script writers. He was an actor and could deliver the message because he had always worked from a script. It's not the same for us. There was never a script for one-on-one doctor-patient conversations. It reminds me of the lack of emphasis in communication skills in my early years of surgical practice, and learned in spades in the later career when I served for many years on the Quality of Medical Performance Committee of provincial and the hospital regulatory bodies. Many of the complaints about physicians by patients arose as a result of failure to explain, failure to take the time to answer questions, and assumptions that people understood what one was saying, when in fact they didn't. It all takes time, truth and syntax! It may reflect a caring attitude if you communicate wisely, but it is more relevant that the patient is truly informed, for the benefit both of the caregiver as well as themselves! It means seeing somewhat fewer patients in a day. There is no available scriptwriter to bail one out. We used to laughingly joke, "We were taught in third year Medicine to write illegibly so that no one could use our records against us; and taught in fourth year Medicine how to mumble so no one could gainsay what we told them!" The joke was, of course, that we ended up with no communication skills. Sometimes that joke, in reality, was not far off. I have seen many cases of superb treatment provided to people who bitterly complained about the treatment because the communication, both before or after treatment, was awful, non-existent, or misunderstood. Since I went to Medical School in the '50s and trained in surgery in the early '60s, communication efforts always took second place at that time to technical skill. I hesitate to even say communication skills, since there is not much skill required, frankly, to spend the time and effort to ensure the patient really understands what they are getting into. It's only fair. The "cared for" in the early days of medical practice were patients, not clients, and certainly not customers. That terminology is evolutionary. We cared deeply in the olden days about doing good work, and since we worked so hard we wondered why they didn't love us. The idea of the patient participating in their care or contributing was nonexistent in those days, even if the doctor was not a martinet. It's hard to even fathom that attitude now, but the change of patient, to client, to customer, for better or worse, is the great leveler. Patients today have better education, internet availability, a pervasive sense of entitlement, and lawyers; it behooves all physicians to communicate well, setting aside the obvious, which is, that it's only fair and the right thing to do! Certainly, like all else, nothing is cut and dried. Respect is a two-way street, and education for everyone is the key!

Dorothy and Martha

Dorothy and Martha were two Labrador Retrievers I spent a year with in 1960. They were used as experimental subjects for my project: the determination of the effect of hypertensive agents on cellular exchange of potassium and sodium. The dog lab was at the University of British Columbia. At that time, UBC had a large attached farm and I would pick up Martha from the kennels on Tuesday and Dorothy on Thursday. They were well looked after in the kennels because they needed to remain healthy throughout the period of experimentation. A conflict I wrestled with was the need to reconcile my desire for a Master's Thesis with the love I had for dogs. When I picked them up, they always seemed to know which day was their day, and after a little quivering they would come with me down the trail, clearly ambivalent, since they enjoyed the time out in the un-kenneled world with an interlude before the day's trial. That they loved me was obvious, which ensured that I always felt like a shit on the experimental day. I am however, good at practicing both sympathy and denial, a useful characteristic in surgery. My predecessor had spent a year teaching both dogs to lie still and semi-supine on a table for 4 to 5 hours while they were cannulated in the femoral artery and two veins, infused with inulin, injected with hypertensive agents, arterial pressures measured, and blood sampled over the period, all the while un-anaesthetized and unrestrained. I have often thought of Dorothy and Martha, and still do now, 52 years later. I think they were precious. I suppose that is sentimental! I don't care. That year was my only prolonged encounter with animal experimentation, thank goodness. In some curious fashion, they were attached to me despite the pain and discomfort I must have inflicted on them, which they bore in silence. At the end of the day, we always had a little play and they gave me tail-wagging affirmation. I suppose even painful attention is better than no attention in the permanently kenneled. Though animal experimentation, even then, went through rigorous ethics assessment and is the heartbeat of scientific progress, the feelings I have today are mixed with the sense of man's inhumanity to dog. I wonder what they will say to me in the hereafter, when I ask their forgiveness for fooling them.

Anatomy examination

In 1960 my surgical colleague and I were seconded by the Department of Surgery, into the Department of Anatomy at the University of British Columbia for a year. My colleague liked it so much he stayed as an Assistant Professor in Anatomy, but I returned to my surgical training after the year. We were designated Teaching Fellows in Anatomy and taught and assisted the sixty-five first-year medical students that dissected cadavers on Monday, Wednesday and Friday; all long eight-hour days in the dissection room. Keeping to the manual; not letting them forge ahead; not macerating the tissue and getting lost; keeping the human road map clear and avoiding misidentifying the signposts and going down the wrong road. We shepherded them throughout the year. They learned that under the skin we are all of the same clay, except the odd anomalous region where we are not. The famous examination that ushered in a sense of dread in all of them was the spot examination. It was a step off the cliff that produced anticipation anxiety. Sixty-five specimen stations were set up on a quadrangular grouping of tables in a large room; each 2 adjacent stations were manned on the outside of the quadrangle by an invigilator from the teaching staff. A bell rang every 90 seconds to signal that the students had to move to the next numbered station. Aside from the bell, the rustle of their pen on paper, and the scraping of chairs, there was no other sound as they moved around the inside of the quadrangle of tables. The students were penned in like sheep being led to the slaughter. The stations may have contained a bone part to identify, a slide of pancreas with an arrow at an islet of Langerhans, a foramen at the base of the skull, a nerve tagged in a shoulder specimen, and so on. It was not only a test of knowledge, but a test of performance under pressure. I was manning the two stations next to the Department Chair. A student examining a slide in front of the chairman was not wearing a white shirt and tie. I heard the chairman say to the student, "Mr. Doe, students of a medical class that are careless about their dress are likely to be careless about their Medical practice and often do not pass this course!" As this man moved to my station the physical appearance of his distress was so devastating that I realized, at that moment, that a life in the academic community may be too far removed for my core, and wasn't enough for my reality. Him, the casualty: me, the lesson! A surgical career may be rough work, but at least hard-earned humility teaches us that pressure and compassion go hand in hand: otherwise it's at our peril in that milieu!

Necrology

Trust the Medical profession to call an obituary record of physicians 'Necrology'! Necrology is the study of death of tissue. Necrotic tissue is how "remains" are described in completely organic terms. I guess it's reality, but you know, "remains" suggests that the necrotic tissue is just what's left. "The remainder!" It implies there was something else. What went? The Vital Force! Thousands of touchings; millions of seeings and hearings; hundreds of lovings; memories in abundance; connectedness to the Universal! The BC Medical Journal came the other day and I knew 10 of the group that died over the past months fairly well out of the 20 or so physicians listed. That is not surprising given our age. Some of us check the obituaries more frequently than others to stay in the loop. There is not a contest to see who is going to live the longest, but to eventually acknowledge that, "When you are old you will stretch out your hands and someone else will dress you and lead you where you do not want to go." That was not just Peter's future predicted, but is the case for most of us as well. The careful, who get to a ripe old age, may go like Oliver Wendell Holmes', The Wonderful One Hoss Shay. If we are still well enough to plead, we may be like blind Teiresias (the one from O Brother, Where Art Thou; not the Greek) on the pump jigger singing, "O Death, won't you spare me over for another year?"—Apostle, Physician or Seer, better be prepared. Those of us who practiced medicine for many years may fight against it, but in fact we accepted death at work as a norm in our patients and ourselves. It may come as a great surprise to most patients and families, and yet the average "in hospital" death rate varies from 2.1% to 5% depending on factors such as hospital and service intensity levels, age corrected criteria, etc. Most people prepare for a new birth with all the paraphernalia for the newborn well in advance, not knowing exactly the time of arrival, but wanting to be ready. There can't be anything more important than the passage into a new life and the preparation of family to welcome the new Force Vitale! The passage out of the old life to "God knows where" has the same immensity. Why then do so many of us fail to get ready in the same way and operate by denial? I guess, like Peter, we probably do not want to be led where we do not want to go. Like Teiresias, we hope to defer for another year. Some hope, like the One Hoss Shay, to remain in perfect shape for a hundred years, then to fall apart all at once, clutching our letter from the Queen. I'm afraid Necrology is just a little too organic a term for me. Pathology not withstanding, 'remains' suggests there is more to it all than just tissue.

Death of the Autopsy

In the decades of the '50s, '60s, and '70s, the autopsy rate gradually diminished until, at the present time, the indication for postmortem examination is largely confined to forensic reasons resulting often from inquests, or sudden unexplained death within 24 hours of hospital admission. Autopsy is almost always ordered by the coroner or court. Why this particularly useful examination has been discarded, as it was used as a frequent assessment of the quality of patient care in the past, can be surmised in the light of several reasons. Autopsies were used as an overview of disease and disorders in diagnosis and treatment, and as a teaching tool in clinical-pathological conferences to enlarge the diagnostic acuity of the clinicians and students. Many clinicians attended the autopsy of their patients to see the what they had found or overlooked. Despite the reasons it was useful, we have trouble claiming an unbroken opportunity to pursue all avenues of evidence-based science in the interest of developing continuing patient care. I am sure that my practicing colleagues would say, "We welcome more autopsies!" Still, there are pragmatic reasons routine autopsies are not more frequently done. It may be that the deceased's family is unwilling to have their loved one's body subjected to autopsy for purely scientific reasons. Hospitals on tight budgets are unwilling to add further expense that would compromise immediate patient needs. There is an acute shortage of pathologists and a complete autopsy is very time-consuming. The provincial governments are unwilling to increase the funding allocation for non-treatment expenses. Physicians erroneously believe the sophisticated imaging of today is a satisfactory replacement for a comprehensive autopsy, or at least good enough as a routine. Physician and hospital liability insurance companies would be reluctant parties to expanded autopsies that might increase the number of litigants based on hitherto uncovered live data. All these factors come into play and evidence-based science is the loser as a result. And so, in fact, is the patient in the end. Good medical care still widely exists in this country where fully-informed, consented to, risk taking medicine by physicians is practiced, rather than cherry-picking only safe cases and off-loading or avoiding the more risky or troubling cases. I still remember with fondness the cut and thrust of the clinical pathology conference with the clinician pitted against the pathologist. The clinician attempted a rational assessment of a selected and illustrative patient, previously unknown to the clinician , but relying only on all the clinical records available in the bright glare of their colleagues and students, thereby exposing their diagnostic acumen or lack thereof, before the autopsy findings were finally revealed in the end by the pathologist. What a way to learn to think systematically and still acquire useful humility! Never fear to be wrong.

The Whole Truth

Quite a few years ago in Lotus City I was on call for Orthopedics at the Royal Jubilee Hospital. They called about a newly arrived patient with recurrent back pain that needed to be seen. It was a case that didn't need to be seen that evening, at least not urgently as further investigations were being done and he was being admitted to the ward. There was an upcoming program on TV I was anxious to see and I looked at my watch and knew if I hustled down, then I could be back in time for my program and I thought I might as well see him in Emergency, though the Emergency room physician said there was no rush.. On the drive to the hospital I heard a siren behind me and pulled over. The policeman came to my window and said "Do you know how fast you were going in a 50k zone?" "No." I said.—"Sir", he said, "You were doing 75k. What's the emergency?"—I said, "I'm a doctor and I was going to the Royal Jubilee Emergency department."— "Can I see your licence?" he asked. After examining it he took out his phone and called his dispatcher. "Find out if Dr. J Warren is expected urgently at Jubilee Emergency", he asked. The dispatcher confirmed that was the case. "Follow me doc", he said, and put his lights and siren on and we wheeled off to the hospital! When I parked he waved, gave me the thumb up, smiled and left! When I went in to the emergency ward, I felt sheepish! Worse, I took advantage of someone! The staff knew, and I knew! They smiled knowingly. I bent my head and shuffled to the patient. I didn't lie to the policeman. I told the truth and I told nothing but the truth, but I didn't tell the whole truth. I could have told him, "I was racing to see a patient that needed seeing, but not urgently. I was told I could see him tomorrow." I told the whole truth to myself though, since you can't fib to the inner man. The urgency was in my interest. You also can't fib to the emergency nurses either, though they will cover for you. I can't tell why I remember little things like this, but it is a form of a lie when we leave out the bits that round out the truth and fail to tell it like it really is!

Fibrotic Creep

A boiling fowl is tough because of fibrotic creep. Someone might say of an elderly eclectic gentleman, "He is a tough old bird!" That someone is literally, righter than they know. I hope no one says of the elderly eclectic gentleman that he is a fibrotic creep. We are all subject to this phenomenon of creep as we become analogous to our boiling cousin, the old rooster! Muscle fibers, which have no real capacity to regenerate, are crept into and replaced by fibrous strings of collagen, replacing over a lifetime both voluntary, involuntary and cardiac muscle fibers. Healthy fat cells providing energy storage, heat, and insulation are emptied of their contents by Father Time and move to fibrous tissue replacement with the losses of fat cells and their function. Bones and joints become brittle with the loss of mineral and relative increase of the fibrous tissue replacing cartilage and bone. Toughened fibrous tissue surrounds the joints and the loss of resilience limits one's range of motion. Gravity flattens the feet which become longer and wider and the fibers around the joints stretch and are painful. If you take a Petri dish and a batch of primitive mesenchymal cells and subject them to varying oxygen tension and varying motion applications, these undifferentiated cells have the capacity to metamorphose. In the young these become fibroblasts, chondroblasts, or osteoblasts, the precursors of fibrous tissue, cartilage or bone, differentiated by the experimental milieu you have created for them! This elegant system, when operating at prime of life, has the capacity to restructure and regenerate, on demand, fibrous tissue, cartilage or bone. If the milieu is changed to low oxygen and low motion, the homeostatic state of the old, excess fibrosis ensues. Those primitive mesenchymal cells form the basis of the framework for our body that in turn houses the vital cells of organs. There is a hourglass at work that spells the demise of the capacity of the magnificent primitive mesenchyme to differentiate selectively. It is gradual but relentless as fibrotic creep invades the spaces of the vital organ cells, as well as the timbers that house them! Paradoxically, we become both tough and feeble; tough and yet, often more tender. Succulent chicken and young Turks: in time all become like boiling fowl!

All Joking Aside

Out of interest, I traveled once to an alternative therapies conference on back pain. It was an interesting experience to listen to the diverse opinions and the seriousness with which the proponents of the various treatments described their results. At a break in the conference for lunch, I was seated next to a young woman practitioner of a discipline with which I was not familiar. We engaged in a short conversation as she seemed very pleasant and was surprised when I told her I was a medical doctor. She said, "Pardon me for saying this, but why is it that medical doctors' handwriting is so illegible?"—"Well," I said, "it's because we are taught to write badly. In second year medicine the course, 'How to Write Bad 201' is taught."—"How can that be?" she said credulously. I waited for a glint of humour in those eyes, but it didn't appear. "Well," I said, piling it on, "we then can't be held responsible for what we write, since no one can read it but us!"—"Good heavens," she said, "I didn't know that!" I looked for any sign of amusement, but there was none to be found in that serious mien. Up the ante was my way to deal with the matter. Surely in that stretch she would see I was joking! "Yes," I said, "and in the course in third-year medicine, 'How to Mumble 301', we complete the skill set 'How to communicate without doing so'. That way we avoid any trouble such as 'You said this or that.'"—"Well," she said as she rose from the table, "I'm glad you told me that!" I could see that I was in deep trouble. She didn't get it. My humour fell flat. To disavow it now would be disingenuous and reaffirm what she wished to believe, possibly, in the first place. I had just trashed myself and medicine in the face of an attempt at ill-advised humour in the wrong arena. I could imagine the furtive looks of disgust from the assembly of conference attendees in the coffee hour later. I slunk away and listened to the rest of the meeting in the shadows. As so many of my loved ones have said to me before, "Why can't you ever be serious for once?"

Shake Your Head!

The last safe opportunity for us to be publicly uncouth was the Freshman Parade in downtown Winnipeg in September 1953. My friend Larry, Mel and I were appointed by the class as the parade committee for the Medical float of that year. The theme of each float was to reflect, in some way, the ethos of each faculty to which we were about to become engaged. Let the gestating Engineers hang Volkswagens from bridges, the Aggies sit on their straw bales and milk a plastic cow—our float was the Sex Machine in full production. To allocate the portrayal of the dignity and image of Medicine, proceeding down Portage Avenue in parade, to a callow group of youths just admitted and not yet baptized in the rigor of the course, must have shaken the heads of the faculty. Having interviewed, in the past two years, applicants for Medicine at UBC, I saw the quality of goodness and mercy, at least as the candidates portrayed themselves, bore no resemblance to the less inhibited attitude we displayed. The past seems scary to me now. Christine Jorgensen, once George Jorgensen, was the first person publicly known to have had a sex change operation. The procedure, an amputation and vaginoplasty, was done in February 1953, and she was an instant celebrity from then on. Taking advantage of a topical idea, we thought it was timely, edgy, and colourful enough to win the first prize for the best float in the parade. Our advantage was that two members of our class were identical twins. One would enter the Sex Machine dressed as a man and the other twin would immediately walk through the exit on the other side, dressed as a woman. The committee had a great time building the sex machine out of plywood on a flat bed truck and then got carried away and embellished it with levers and wheels with all sorts of dirty labels describing the surgical activity within the box. This was augmented by fireworks and smoke issuing forth from the machine throughout the duration of the parade. Rather than winning a prize for the float, we were castigated by the Winnipeg Free Press for unbecoming behavior and immorality. My mother called it smutty. Curiously, we were never sanctioned by the senior Medical Faculty, though we did receive a significant series of lectures on ethics, dignity and grace necessary to bring to the practice of Medicine. Thank goodness for me, in 1953 the entrance criterion was entirely based on marks. There was no interview process for putative medical students at that time. I suppose the possibility of taking raw material, intelligent, but still in the stage of a lump of clay, demonstrably human and unrestrained, callow, but too naïve to be dishonest, may have posed an interesting challenge for faculty. Better possibly the students that would have been too dumb to lie, than some who are exceptionally facile during the interview. Still, I do have to shake my head.

Cross Fertilization

For the training period of specialization in any field, the focus toward acquisition of a skill requires commitment to all the elements that comprise the specialty. That is not only true, but it is self-evident. It is abundantly clear that the more time, effort and applied intelligence is availed will result in greater knowledge of the elements needed for superior performance. Narrowing the field of specialization will enable the individual to seek and find higher and deeper planes of information leading to super-specialized knowledge on a narrowing base, and more and more unique capabilities, but often, as a result, individuals find themselves bound to the tree or maybe the branch, rather than the forest. There are few of us in medicine who have the capacities of Lister and Osler. In the practice of orthopedic surgery for instance, the knowledge base of generalized medicine and surgery precedes the specialization in order to give a sound foundation to the surgical decision-making. Embarking then on progressively exclusive specialization diminishes the time available to continue to renew the broader knowledge base, a base in which much changes dramatically every decade. Yesterday's received wisdom is today's history! The fragmentation of medical specialties and subspecialties necessarily sacrifices general knowledge for specific knowledge. Yesterday's concept of the idealized orthopedic surgeon could be exemplified by my written examination for Fellow of the Royal College of Surgeons of Canada (Orthopedics) of 1963. I say this not to recommend it, but to show the degree of altered emphasis apparent at that time. The written exam was on four topics, given equal importance: 1) The causes of Essential Hypertension 2) Fractures of the Tibia 3) The mechanism of Renal Tubular Absorption 4) The Embryology of the Spinal Cord. To be granted a Fellowship was said then to have achieved both specific and a broader knowledge. We can't have it all now. In the forty years of orthopedic surgery that I participated in, the progressive narrowing of an individual's scope applied to his field of work was necessary in order to maintain the skill-set in an era of rapid progression of knowledge. The value of INTRA-specialty team practice is provided by a closely-knit group practice.

Working intimately together allows for greater discovery from shared insights. The value of new insights provided by INTER-specialty close surgical relationships is often not taken advantage of with the pressure of time, but is a potent source of discovery often under-utilized. I believe that the ideal surgical model for maintenance of excellence is threefold, granted equal skill and knowledge brought in at the beginning of one's surgical career, keeping, as Sir William Osler alluded to, the wind in your sail.

1. Close knit group practice in the chosen specialty fostering ongoing learning from the INTRA-specialty interaction leading to cross-fertilization.

2. Progressive narrowing of the scope of practice of each individual to maintain skill with aging.

3. Closer connections with the wider range of medical specialties, fostering ongoing learning from INTER-specialties contact, leading to relevant generalized cross-fertilization.

These observations for cross-fertilization of course are not unique to medicine but apply doubtless to many highly technical fields in which rapid change occurs.

Gait and Posture

I once considered surreptitiously taking videos of my medical colleagues as part of a proposed study of posture and gait. Normal variants of gait and posture in healthy people are of some interest to those of us concerned with musculoskeletal anatomy and physiology! The long hospital corridors would allow me to record individuals whose gait and posture were identifiers. The good orthopedic surgeon was always aware of the need to observe the patient walking, sitting and standing as part of their assessment. One of the most interesting clinical games we used to play was the single Walk Through. Pathological cases with gait or postural abnormalities were diagnosed as they passed in front of us, once, at normal pace. We could identify osteoarthritis hip or knee, below knee amputation, stone in shoe, spinal stenosis and much else; it was a chance to shine, when we could diagnose a limp triumphantly over one's colleagues. The nature of involuntary gait and posture, normal and pathological, is as unique as a fingerprint. For years, I idly considered writing a paper on the subject of normal variants; now it's too late. In retrospect, it seems it may have been too intrusive to my colleagues. Still, I fondly remember examples I might have used for my unborn paper! For instance, in the matter of healthy gaits, Dr. S was heavily muscled in the hips and walked with a sideways lurch, broaching like a boat taking wind and wave on the quarter. He had reverse Trendelenberg's signs due to strong gluteus medius muscles and looked either like an uncomfortable boat or a farm boy walking home in two furrows. Drs. X and Y had short heel cords. A short but strong Tendo Achilles leads to a bouncy gait. The stride has high amplitude, so more push-off energy is required to achieve the same stride distance. X and Y would make poor waiters or, in another era, bad footmen. They would break dishes or spill the food. A lax Tendo Achilles would lead to a low amplitude, gliding gait. One might say, "No spring in his step! Good waiter material!" Dr. Z had a military officer background. He stood erect and his head and eyes were directed upward to heaven as he marched down the hall. His gait and posture had an ethereal quality! One didn't like to interrupt him since he always seemed visionary, gazing above at new horizons. What was a learned gait and posture from his service training became imprinted and involuntary. Drs. A and B were topmost physicians and mild enemies. Nevertheless, they often required to speak of professional matters as they met in the hall. As they stood and talked of weighty matters, practically linked together at the groin, they slowly rotated to the right in tandem, as it were, torquing and talking to what they thought was the most vulnerable side of one another, simultaneously! Pushmepullyou! The more florid variations of gait and posture are the most interesting, but all of us have unique physical characteristics providing a wide range of normal that is recognizable from a distance. — She saw him coming from a long way off and though afar, recognized his walk, the cadence, the swing of the arms, finally coming home for good, so raced down the road to him, tears of joy streaming down her face!

Cheating

Avoiding pitfalls in university exams includes sidestepping opportunities to cheat. The temptation to do so is occasionally present in a competitive environment, when we were trying to get the marks necessary to get into and to stay in Medicine. I escaped the pitfall twice in my student years, largely through cowardice, I must confess, rather than any surge of ethics. In my pre-med year, my marks were good since I needed them to transfer to the medicine faculty. A colleague; not a friend, but a playboy and bon vivant in my pre-med year and also an occasional drinking companion, knew that I was heading to good marks in invertebrate zoology, and asked me to write his exam for him. He offered me fifty dollars to do it: a big sum in 1953. I told him no, mostly because of cowardice, but also self-righteousness since he never bothered to spend any time at the subject. I don't really think at that time I had any strong ethical sense. I just was cautious about being found out and risking the destruction of my budding career. The second time was in second year medicine when my friend, in first year medicine, gave me a prepared copy of the final second year bacteriology exam two days before the examination. Once in my hand it was difficult not to look at it. There was no question on it that I couldn't have answered easily. However, paranoid though I may be, I think in retrospect I was being set up for disaster. I was a good student in bacteriology, but I wasn't a great student in that course. A laboratory technician, whose wife had been trying to seduce me, had left a copy of the examination questions "inadvertently" near my friend's library table in the evening. My friend couldn't help but notice it and was impelled to show me. What to do? I had no way out. I solved the problem by writing the exam badly enough that I could get by without detection while kicking myself at the same time. Cowardice however has a place in all of this. Had I taken great umbrage, and asked for a separate exam since I had seen a copy, the shit would have hit the fan for everyone but me. Thanks to my cowardice, no one lost their job, no one was exposed for cheating, no one was expelled for passing information about exams, and I was never seduced, probably again because of cowardice and naivety rather than ethics. There is no doubt that growing up in the prairie boondocks you may have been a naif but at least had to look where you were going to avoid stepping in fresh cow pies.

Busy Hands

In the olden days when my children were teenagers, from time to time when lassitude struck and indolence lurked around the corner, I would observe the axiom that, "Busy hands are happy hands!" It was and is a tenet of faith I carry, but of course they would respond immediately by gagging motions into an imaginary barf bag. I expected such a response, of course, but we had communicated and they knew it, though it became sort of a joke, (CBS) Corny But Satisfactory. I was astounded to get a communication from the Royal College of Physicians and Surgeons of Canada the other day with information that we had unemployed Orthopedic surgeons, Neurosurgeons and Cardiac surgeons, newly graduated, that couldn't find places to work in Canada now. The cream of the crop that we can't seem to fit in after all that training and available skill were not being utilized to the fullest here. One of the most satisfying aspects of my career in Lotus City was being part of the recruitment and utilization of young Orthopedic surgeons; one added to our roster every three to four years throughout most of the past thirty years. They added greatly to the health of our Service with the contribution of current knowledge and new skills. Rather than competition, the addition of these surgeons increased the energy of all and confirmed the adage that busy hands are indeed happy hands. Rationing of health care in this country by governments may save money, but is it worth it in the face of inordinately long waiting lists, inadequate expansion of high tech facilities, and unwillingness to address the antiquated Canada Health Act for fear of political suicide? The slow erosion will continue. Where is today's Edmund Burke when we need him? He may have been turfed by the electors of Bristol after a single term, but he lives on in our minds and literature and had self respect, while many of the politicians of his day, easily manipulated by both the caucus and constituents, maybe reelected, but in time were never heard about again. Burke always spoke and voted his own mind and paid the price. My long association with surgeons has taught me this: these brothers and sisters under the skin would work for practically nothing if the tool shop was excellent and the team was topnotch. Money is not the big issue; it is the side issue, although the money is good. I too am aware. of the overall major costs these particular surgeons generate secondarily for the health care budget. But let's face it! Health care Delayed is Health care Denied! In the operating theatre, "Busy Hands are Happy hands!"

NEUROSIS

Phytophagiacs

When my father read the newspaper in the olden days, he often absentmindedly tore off corners of the newspaper and chewed and swallowed them as he ate up and absorbed the news of the day. Cellulose is as indigestible as the news is, both in those days, and perhaps even more so today! Phytophagy (cellulose eating) can occasionally morph into the compulsion to eat plant matter unselectively and pathophysiology ensues if the matter is indigestible like cellulose. Those persons who compulsively eat large volumes of cellulose are diagnosed as Phytophagiacs. The activity leaves a growing mass of cellulose, which over time, by accretion, becomes a Phytobezoar. This ball of cellulose is trapped in the stomach since it becomes too big to enter into the narrow area of the gastrointestinal tract beyond! A little like a wet snowball that rolls down the hill getting bigger and bigger until it hits the narrow mountain pass and obstructs all travelers. My dad never ate enough that it accumulated! Since he rarely read books, our stock of books was unmarked! One always knew that he had read the paper or the magazine, however, from the absent corners. It was an act like the neighborhood dog idly pissing on the hydrant, marking the territory, or like Kilroy, here for a visit and leaving his chalk mark that he was here. For some reason, I suppose heredity, I continued his habit, idly tearing the odd corner off a book and chewing it as I ingested the material and its content. It was never bad enough for it to be considered a pica, but it offended my friends if I had borrowed their book! Cellulose from paper is one thing, but wooden matches, toothpicks, popsicle sticks and other wood bits are worse. Human beings are not beavers. When I first married the pianist she was horrified to see the ingestion of her books, corner by corner as I sought to absorb her interesting reading material! I realize now,. it was a form of marking, claiming ownership, territorial affirmation, however unconsciously and innocently done! A habit idly acquired is easily dispensed with in the interest of literary harmony, when love intervenes! I no longer have ever gone back to that bad habit. When my son grew up, became a bibliophile and had his own library, I often read his books and carefully avoided eating the corners, but for a while, bent open the spines of his tighter books for easier reading. Again, I was castigated for my destructive tendencies towards books. I am careful now to eat candy or popcorn when I read, and strain to read obliquely through a semi-open book if it is newish and not my own! I want to be good and avoid the sins of the fathers!

The Polluter

The pianist and I have a 1990 Nissan Axxess that is in good running order, partly because it is softly used and serviced regularly. I tried to start it the other day after we had been away for a while and the battery had run down since a ceiling light had been left on. When the tow truck man came and jumped the battery, he told me to run it for a half hour to charge up the battery. I drove around Lotus Island for a while with the pianist and then took her to her bank. I was fearful about turning off the ignition at that stage, so I sat in the car with it running in idle while she did her business. I was musing on nothing in particular when a small, purpose-driven lady in earth clothing came over and said, "You people are all the same. You pollute the earth with your gas fumes and use up a natural resource and do not have any regard for the earth or the people in it." She was quiet and intense, and having made her clear statement she left me hanging and crossed back over the road. I wondered, "Am I of the tribe of 'You People' and who are 'You People' anyway?" I was never given the chance to explain that I was not one of 'Them.' A man then emerged from the bank wearing earth clothes and came to my open window and said, "You know your car is running!" — "Yes," I said, "My battery is flat and I am afraid to turn it off as yet since it is still charging and I may not get it started again." — "That's OK then," he said. I thought, "Thanks a lot green buddy." It is not that I was being accosted and taken to task that took me aback so much, since this is Lotus Island. It's just that I am named one of the 'You People,' separated, categorized, held up as a lesson and packaged as an "Other". It's hard for all of us, me too, not to jump to conclusions!

Coinage Redux

I'm trying to turn over a new leaf but I am too embarrassed to go to the bank. It's been my habit for years to either pay for purchases with a credit card, or pay with paper currency. The credit card, because it's an interest-free loan for a few days, or paper currency because I hate standing in line while someone at the cash register counts and recounts, out loud, a volume of coinage from a purse! Coin passers are good and faithful financial stewards, no doubt, but since I am impatient and have time anxiety I would be embarrassed to hold the people up behind me if I doled out my dimes and nickels in that fashion. In addition, a man's wallet is rarely designed for coinage. Can I imagine those people waiting in line thinking, "That fellow is a frugal and exemplary character that is careful with his coinage and to be commended for the careful financial stewardship he seems to display?" No, I can't! They are thinking, "What kind of a guy has a wallet with a big change purse, or alternatively capacious pockets in his trousers that are so misshapen with heavy coinage he carries around that his pockets are wrenched out of shape and his trousers sag so badly they may descend below his buttocks." I admit the unreasonable coin hang-up I have, has, in the past, lead to sequestered loose coinage over the years in Ziploc bags in my sock drawer, the basement work shelf, the photograph cupboard, filing cabinet and sundry other places. Ziploc inventory was an organizational start to my new leaf, as prior to the Ziploc storage it was loose change in every nook and cranny in every room in the house. The pianist finally said "Deal with it or else!" So I gave some thought to tubing my coins in accurate tally to take to the bank: pennies, nickels, dimes, quarters and loonies. I haven't done it yet, but I'm working toward it. I'm waiting until the bank seems empty! Those coins have lost much value over the years with currency devaluation and I have no one to blame except myself for my ill-advised attempts to avoid coin passing! I am going to recycle my soon-to-disappear pennies as well from now on, but I just need a bolt of courage. So if you are in a hurry to get home, and have to get to the washroom as well, from now on I feel for you, but cross your legs in the bank or grocery lineup, I am doing what counts and it is taking a lot out of me! I'm not classy enough to avoid carrying money and only buy at my club. I don't even have a club. I'm too old to get a man bag, but if I did I would feel sillier than I already do.

Adjustment Disorder

Adjustment Disorder, a healthy, temporary, self-limiting condition, is my diagnosis of myself, based on a move from our waterside farm to an urban townhouse in Lotus Island. It is, at the moment, worse than retirement from a job I loved. It is worse than the adjustment from wellness to Rheumatoid arthritis. Our friends, our social life, and activity of a voluntary nature is unchanged, but at the townhouse I am still lost for stimulation. It has been six months and counting. It's not depression, but more bewilderment. I am still sulking. The nature of the farm, which I immersed myself in for 32 years and which gave me a thrill every morning as Mother Nature greeted me anew each day, and which kept me busy, has been lost. I believe the rational thing the pianist and I have done by moving was supremely correct. I could no longer manage the farm physically. The cost of hiring help for things I was always able to do for myself in the past was demeaning and prohibitive for old age pensioners. The fault was all mine since I created a labour-intensive garden in which I could not bear to watch the cracks develop. The townhouse we have moved to is beautiful and affordable. I, however, forgive myself entirely for my feelings of ennui, despite the fact that I could blame myself for being incredibly spoiled. What the heart feels, the head must understand, since the organism needs its balance in life. Homeostasis! I will float on this un-riffled sea of relatively imposed vacuity until I know where to go! There is no urgency. I am resolved now to do what enthuses me for the rest of my life. Aught will change my mind! No more oughts! There have been so many oughts in the past. So many oughts spearheaded by guilt! So many oughts designed by my inability to say no and my desire to fill in a day. Maybe I will learn to say no graciously. Many things I have agreed to do in the past that were burdensome, I did badly, or forgot to complete and ended up feeling a failure as a result. I don't want that feeling any more. If I am not enthused about it, I am not going to do it, risking a scent of narcissism. I think God wants us to value what we do. If it can be done with joy and is also useful and meaningful, so much the better. Though I know the world provides no free lunch, I am going to start quibbling about the price from now on, or look for a better menu. A little like Mary and less like Martha. Self-limiting disorders like this end when the self finally decides to limit the disorder.

Beerbelly-Spindleshanks

The middle-aged males in my paternal line have slid into this physique with or without the benefit of beer and chips and despite adequate physical activity. It's DNA, all the way! I have to confess in my family, that strong drink was welcome and that Shank's Mare always gave way to the horse as a form of transport, but the anatomy of our middle-aged forebears, from all the generational photos, it appears ,was a bond handed down from our distant Irish family's Y chromosomes. Some years ago I was walking from the pre-anesthetic room, as a patient for a change, down the corridor to the operating room in one of those skimpy little gowns that demonstrate everything you never wanted all the world to see with the flapping backside open to the breeze. The nurses were all my friends and therefore were licensed to be rude, as are all who care for you! They had all assisted me in the Orthopedic OR for years and were delighted to see me punished in the gown and horizontal rather than vertical. One of my favorites of the nurse assistants said, "You know, when you are walking, especially in short flappy gowns, with your skinny legs, you look like a fat man being carried by a chicken!" Another said, "You're luffing on your windward side." It rolled off my back since I have always given as good as I got over the years, and if it gave them all pleasure I didn't want to deny them that. Even at a younger age I was never a flat bellied, six pack man, with legs like tree trunks. I carried rather the family's signal physique! I belonged and so did most of my brothers! When you have good friends or family that love you or love to be with you, there is a joyous opportunity to engage the license to be rude. We would like to be long-lived, but only as long as the price is that it doesn't seem to be too long. It's too late to correct the spindleshanks, but probably is within one's grasp to modify the beer belly without denial or masking of one's allegiance to the features of one's own breed! I still want to fully belong. If I provide an opportunity to regale my confreres, it is only low comedy and I carry the family flag with pride of place.

Moisture

Scrub your hands and bottom best
And treat with gentleness the rest.

The hype of the skin moisturizers and their pitches about skin care have prompted me to attack the whole idea for the 95% of people who have healthy skin, since the pitch claims are in fact almost solely cosmetic! The television ads undermine the natural, and promote plasticity in human beings! I am not a dermatologist, but I do have common sense and know this: that Mother Nature is never wrong, and Ockham's Razor is usually right! The fetish of bathing or showering once or twice a day, robbing one's epidermis by scouring off Mother Nature's lipids, wax esters, glycerides, squalene, and sialomucin, all its natural sebum oils, and then, when one has finally denuded their epidermis of this protective coating, adding some cream that smells like a flower, resists Vitamin D and is manufactured from the petroleum industry, is an act of violation! The natural epidermal ooze is much more complex than I have elaborated, but one came with it in abundance when we traversed the birth canal with our lipid covering of vernix caseosa! It accumulated in utero and protected us. We are still protected now if we allow it to remain in a modest way. It's not that one shouldn't bathe at all; it's just that it is badly overdone. I guess it's reasonable to smell like a flower some of the time, but the erotic scent of the healthy hominid will always trump the erotic scent of everyone smelling inhuman. Even your dog will celebrate your natural scent. The dermatological scientists can't agree on the specific utility of all these natural waxy coatings we have been provided with, but human beings should still smell like people and retain their natural waxes and oils minus the dirt. The coating is there for a reason. Not knowing the whole of the role they supply doesn't count! Mother Nature is always right, and the correct answer, according to William of Ockham, is usually the simplest answer! Soap and water and a fresh towel is the sexy answer for the natural hominid, then and now. Moreover, everyone is going to look like they really look like! That'll be interesting. Let's not get plastered too often! Lets not stay in the sun endlessly for our squamous cells sake. Lets not worry about being white or wrinkled. Let's agree that added kind of beauty may be not even skin deep.

Mummies Blankets

At the risk of being considered a sissy by those of hard-nosed countenance, I have a paean to offer. The pianist and I use on our beds today the blankets our mothers made for us about 25 years ago. They are used by us in praise, remembrance and as a talismanic connection to the past. The pianist's blanket her mother made was a soft blue, brown and white in a zigzag pattern: strictly uniform, crocheted, crisp and perfectly preserved. My mother's was a looser, block knit, tan, brown and orange with a touch of white and tasseled. Both are beautifully finished as could be expected from these women in their late '80s at that time. My blanket is smaller than the pianist's since my mother was more impatient, so would have quit earlier in the process, in order to do other things. The blanket, for the bed and chair, gives warmth, comfort, and an embrace that reflects what they, as women, gave to us, along with the continuity to the past the blankets still provide. When I look at these blankets today they are entirely representative of the personalities of the two women and a more accurate display than words can express. If they could look down today they would smile at the blankets they prized and left us. When my mother provided me with my satin smooth blanket in infancy that I used until I was three, it was my talisman; it was her breast when I slept alone, and it gave me comfort. The pianist and I can still celebrate the presence of our mothers today with the continuation of our preserved crocheted and knitted blankets. Why did I not realize that the many years of my life after three was so dangerous till I rediscovered my mother's gift in my latter years and was safe again? What incredible dangers the pianist and I encountered during those times in life where we neglected to credit blanket power. It's never too late to learn anew, what you only knew as an infant! Safe at last!

Time Anxiety

My mother and her twin sister would meet my grandfather at 5 pm at Portage and Main, in Winnipeg, and the girls would get a ride home to Little Britain each night. In the winter, Portage and Main resembled Greenland! My mother was at Normal School on the Pembina campus on the way to a teacher's certificate, and my aunt in Medical School on the Bannatyne campus. If they were late in arriving, my grandfather would leave them behind and drive home on his own. They would then have to take the streetcar, north to the end of the line and transfer to the infrequent Selkirk bus. They had to travel 20 odd kilometers all told by public transport, and would arrive home at 7 or 8 pm; it was a two or three hour journey! Growing up with my mother, I knew she had time anxiety and her constant refrain for any or all appointments where I was hauled along with her was, " Hurry. Hurry. Hurry." It is not within the nature of little boys to hurry, hurry, hurry, but over time these incantations were assimilated. After all, your mother is your mother! And so, inevitably, I also developed time anxiety. It drives the pianist crazy. To lighten the mood, I will play act by pawing the floor like a bull. Since she understands the irrationality, she never plays a taunting hand. Paradoxically, the curious thing about time anxiety I note is that those who have it, often walk close to the edge of their cliff of fear: a self imposed dawdle that confirms, in their own mind, the truth and "reasonable" nature of their unreasonable reaction. You can't fill in your own hole if you're standing in it. Dawdling, followed by anxiety, was characteristic of both my mother and me. We rarely, if ever, missed the appointments, as I recall, but I now know the anxiety was all my grandfather's fault and not my mother's. Me? Now that I know we create it in order to justify it there is no excuse for it any longer.

RELIGION

Mountain Climber

Today is the Feast of the Transfiguration. Those who climb the mountain to the top will be changed if not transformed. To reach the top is not to stay there. The hardest part is to go back into whatever valley you have to deal with, where you wanted to be cool, not entirely giving up and giving in to the new view. The priest today said that some of us may have been at the mountaintop and were transformed. I thought, "I was, I was, my hand is up!" My hand wasn't really up. I'm an Anglican. I looked around carefully at the congregation. I didn't see any hands up. I didn't deserve to get to the mountaintop, but I was placed there by a Holy Helicopter, Circa 1968, Sorrento BC. It was bliss. I felt like a bird with wings for three months and moved with the wind, but was probably considered mildly mad by my surgical colleagues and friends. I may have been dreadfully eager to reach all those I believed were in need, who in fact treated me with compassion, but all the euphoria gradually faded since living on a mountaintop too long addles the brain. Transformed, no; transfigured, no; but changed and slowly adapted, yes. The valley is where we are to live, not the mountain: not Olympus, not Mount of Olives, not the Acropolis, not even the Mount of the Transfiguration. I finally prayed a prayer that the feeling of religious euphoria would leave me because it was interfering with my ability to do my job. Not to worry, some of it sticks and anyway, work and job are not the same. You may be lucky enough to have your string jerked as well, usually after a crisis, which it was for me, but gradualism is the thoughtful and longitudinal way to go. That's just leading to the work part that is demanded of those of us in the valley. Partly blind, partly poor, partly weak, control given over, hardly cool: that's us. The mountain and the valley are symbols. The mountain, illumination—the valley, implementation. Never disparage the power of symbols: a visible manifestation of an invisible idea. When Martin Luther King led the people's march on Washington shortly before his assassination he knew and mentioned that the air was rife with threats against his life. Dr King knew that to be a shepherd to his people was dangerous to the established order. He preached peace, but change.

In his last paragraph he said, "And then I got to Memphis. And some began to say the threats, or talk about the threats that were out. We've got some difficult days ahead. But it doesn't really matter with me now. Because I've been to the mountaintop. I don't mind. Like anybody, I would like to live a long life; longevity has its place. But I'm not concerned about that now. I just want to do God's will. And He's allowed me to go up to the mountain. And I've looked over. And I've seen the Promised Land. I may not get there with you. But I want you to know tonight, that we, as a people, will get to the Promised Land."

Like the Wind

Traveling swiftly through the forest darkling
No broken branch, no twig misplaced
No deep footprints in the wet, no leaf displaced
Silent and swift in unbroken movement
Going somewhere in search of place to place
Observing everything, disturbing nothing
Touching everything, disturbing nothing
Leaving silently, spoiling nothing
Known to You alone

A Good Man

I recently read a column in the National Post by Barbara Amiel in which she mentioned Septimus Harding in passing. He is one of my favorite characters in fiction and a subject that figures large in Anthony Trollope's novel, Barchester Towers. He is a prime example of the ordinary as truly extraordinary. The fabric of the novel clearly displays the seven cardinal sins, shown in relief in the carefully-crafted clergy, but throughout, the threads of this seemingly ordinary man Septimus, appear from time to time, always in the background except at the conclusion. In the BBC film production of Barchester Towers, artistic license was taken, in that the paragraph about Septimus Harding that ends the novel has been moved and placed instead, in the film, as a eulogy provided in an after-dinner toast by his son-in -law, Dr Grantly, the archdeacon. But, as I say again, in the book it is Trollope's own concluding narrative paragraph. Clearly, it is of great importance to Trollope as he takes it upon himself to describe his feelings towards his own creation, rather than the narrative device of using another of his characters to speak for him. Herein goes the paragraph: "The author now leaves him [Harding], in the hands of his readers: not as a hero, not as a man to be admired and talked of, not as a man who should be toasted at public dinners and spoken of with conventional absurdity as a perfect divine, but as a good man without guile, believing humbly in the religion which he has striven to teach, and guided by the precepts which he has striven to learn." One can clearly see why the BBC had to place this wonderful narrative as dialogue in order to include it. One can also see why Trollope is willing to place Septimus Harding at the mercy of his readers. The place in this life of the Septimus Hardings of this world is so obscured by the lurid and extravagant that we cannot see them clearly through the haze. When a master like Trollope brings them to life, we are humbled by their majesty!

Eureka, I think

Whenever the heart gives me a little epiphany and I feel eureka, the head says, "Better think about that first." That's the problem of being human. It's early December now and soon we will sing, We Three Kings. For years, the pianist has played the piano at Christmas with the family clustered around singing the carols and hymns. The carol, 'We Three Kings,' has verses for our clustered individuals to sing and since none of our family sings that well, there is a comedic and awkward character to the individual singers. However, it's fun! The lyrics of the hymn are well known and the gifts the Magi bring are not so much gifts, as tokens, prefiguring the traveler's belief in the nature of the person for whom they have come. Gold for the King, Frankincense for the Priest, Myrrh for the Sacrifice. Symbols that are a recognition, on their part, of what is to come. The hymn leaves no room for human doubt, and though a favorite is a pastiche of Matthew's account. T.S. Eliot's poem, 'Journey of the Magi,' is not complete. It leaves room for us. The Magus who narrates the poem was alone then, reflecting on his journey, and his epiphany, which seems to me, was 'Eureka, I think!' He notes, "it wasn't easy and it wasn't sure and there was doubt." The epiphany for him, both was, and wasn't, a long time coming. The poem stirs the soul because it reflects a thoroughly human person who has to grapple with the same uncertainties that many others and I do. Who provided the great gift? Whose is the gift? That's easy if we and eureka are right. It's the Babe. The narrator of the poem has now the gift of distance and time to arrive at the discovery of the paradox that out of death can come life. Someone said to me, "I don't understand what you mean by that last sentence, 'life out of death.' It doesn't make any sense!" "Well." I said, "Read the poem again! I'm not going to tell you what I think it means. It's not my job. You're not a stupid man so you will have your own ideas and they are as good as mine, though you and I will never be as poetic as Eliot! And we'll never have to ride a thousand miles on a camel in the winter to find out either!"

Boogeyman

Tomorrow is Ash Wednesday and I will meet my Boogeyman. Last night I dreamt of him. He appeared on a flat sea at the horizon; at a distance, a tall hairy Ellipsoid rapidly walking on water toward me with disturbed seagulls flying in the background. It looked initially like a tall hairy dog, and then a burro, and then a young Wilding! The eyes were glistening! He asked me if I was alone! My Boogeyman is the interior evil that manifests from time to time when I don't nourish the goodness and feel alone. Then, not only does the Boogeyman speak for me, but he also closes my ears and appears in my eyes and the mouth and posture, much like the Boogeyman of Dr. Jekyll. Jesus dealt with his Boogeyman three times in the wilderness by obedience to Goodness. It does no good to believe that the interior Boogeyman is not there with me. He is always there. When I went to a silent retreat on Ash Wednesday one time, I was assailed with a dream about my collection of sins: sins of commission and omission. They came falling down from the sky like large raindrops with labels. The recognition of them is liberating in a setting that promotes goodness and forgiveness. When I was a little boy I always looked under my bed to make sure the Boogeyman was not there. He was never there, or anywhere else outside of me. Having now found him, it is possible to keep him more or less in check by suffering through the acknowledgement of both the sins of omission and commission and striving to nourish the goodness, in preparation of Easter Day, when my load and my cross is shouldered anew!

Invitation

If one is reading something, or singing something, and out of the blue a sentence or a lyric smacks you in the face, it may be something powerful that you knew was a truth. What you needed to hear comes from beyond, when you are mystically oriented. This is never something that you sought; that you were aware of, but it appears to have sought you out. Two things happened that day to me! Jean read from Samuel,—"Eli said, 'Go lie down; and if he calls you, you shall say, —"Speak Lord for thy servant hears." ' " Then later, in the singing of the hymn, Worship the Lord in the Beauty of Holiness, I also felt something. The lyric by JSB Monsell reads, "Fear not to enter his courts in the slenderness of the poor wealth thou canst reckon as thine…" Whether a wealth of goodness, or money, or intellect or pedigree, it cuts no spiritual ice today. The church may have, at one time in the past, for a period of time, revered and thrived with the help of wealth and power and prestige, intellect, pedigree and celebrity. That is certainly no longer the case and the church is becoming threadbare. The church as an establishment no longer serves as a network of power to wealth of a certain kind. There are better networks available for those. The church serves to wealth of another kind. My church should no longer long for those symbols of power since the church's credibility amongst the mass of unchurched is two or three generations away from its Communion, and its weakness will be its strength. Churchiness is no longer de rigueur! That is one of the cleansing acts. The prognostications one reads lately, that the Anglican church will die out over the next fifty years, will never happen! There may be a continuing erosion, and more hardship, but the institutional church is only a vehicle, not an entity unto itself. It takes us from here to there. It may not have wheels, but it is a place for travelers. The institution may struggle but the body will stay. Love, hope and charity don't need a roof. They didn't in the Galilee and they don't now. Possibly, we will settle at some time to an irreducible minimum, but there will always be poor people, rich people, distressed people, smart people, caring people, sometime adversaries, those whose door opens, who begin to listen, and who speak to Whom they hear!

The Sexton

As I lie on my reserved plot in the Anglican cemetery on Lotus Island, getting the feel of it; above, the blue sky and cumulus clouds and bright sun that I love, along with the pastoral surroundings of a verdant nature that will be there, as before, when I am underground. For my sins I guess, I am the cemetery manager for the four Anglican cemeteries on Lotus Island where there seems to be more dead Anglicans than live Anglicans these days. This job I suppose makes me a quasi-sexton and the full description of that job says one is the custodian of the sacred objects. Can I think of a more sacred set of objects than the remains of the families' and friends' loved ones? I cannot! To assist with those who choose the plot they wish, to sell it, to organize and be with those who dig, to stand back as the circle of family and the priest inter the remains, and connect with the grief expressed at the outer edge of the circle, becomes an enclosing act of worship, not just for the person interred, but for the event of committal itself. To enter the earth and become the earth is the final act and the final goodbye. As I cover the urn with soil, it still strikes me that the bell tolls for one of us and all of us at that time, as a piece that falls off the promontory, as John Donne noted in his Meditation, the shape of what is left changes. I had no idea my first year as a mini- sexton would teach me so much. I guess it may be true that most, or maybe all of life is just a rehearsal!

Jawbone of an Ass

The mandible of the ass, and our jawbone as well for that matter, is developed from the primitive cartilaginous templates of the mandible in utero, forming on either side in the primitive face. The left and right primitive mandible become united at a symphysis in front, at the point of the chin, which remains cartilaginous for some time after birth and later fuses when ossification completes. Either the left or right half of the mandible of the ass, when detached from its counterpart through the cartilaginous symphysis, becomes a serious curvilinear weapon. No doubt there were vultures that had denuded the face of a young ass with an as yet unfused symphysis in ancient Palestine. Provided a half jawbone for Samson to kill a number of fleeing Philistines in "heaps." Samson had broken the bonds the Philistines had tied him with, and he exacted revenge upon his captors and revenge for their cruelty towards the Israelites with a weapon that was, and is, shaped like a sickle. It may have been used as a sharpened tool to cut grain stalks as well, in this pre-bronze age era! The slaughter was seen, from the oral tradition of the Israelites, as sanctioned by God for the chosen people; later, recorded as Judges 15: 15-16. In the Billy Bob Thornton movie, Sling Blade, the protagonist, Karl Childers, a retarded strongman, protects a desperately abused woman and child who have befriended him, from a pathological abuser they cannot escape, by killing the abusive man with a sharpened lawnmower blade, not dissimilar in shape or function from Samson's tool, a curvilinear instrument to cut grass. Karl had spent many years previously in an asylum for the criminally insane from childhood for an earlier killing of his mother and her illicit lover when he, in ignorance, employed the same "biblical justice" in this act. He used a sling blade at that time, which, again, is like a sickle for cutting grass stalks. He was released as cured from the asylum, but during his captivity, as in the battle of Samson, he heard simple bible stories, took them literally rather than figuratively, and saw truth as black or white. Like Samson, he was bound by the bonds of his simplistic Bronze Age understanding and cast those bonds and his freedom aside to protect helpless people he had come to love. See the movie before you judge! Retribution, violence and justice are nothing new and simple to the simple. Outside or inside the bible or whatever code we follow, we are never free from its justifiable outrage, our dark side, and who could honestly say they could never commit self-justifiable homicide given sufficient provocation arising out of the passions of love and hate! Nothing is ever simple. but we can't escape our primitive.

SURGERY

The Power of One

Some time ago a woman in her mid-seventies was trapped between the doors of an elevator in a parkade. The doors shut when she tripped on entering and both legs and one arm were jammed outside the elevator doors as it ran up four floors and then down again to ground level. She was transferred to the hospital in extremis! The limbs were mutilated. I was working in the OR at the time, just finishing a fractured hip. The general surgeon phoned up from Emergency and asked if I would look after her as I could make a space if I bumped my next case. We examined her in the operating room and her three limbs were multiply fractured; her tissue-shredded open wounds were filled with dirt and ground up with grease. Nothing was salvageable and an ill- informed attempt to do so would be certain death in the face of old kidneys. Immediate removal of irretrievable sources of contaminated crush products from entering the blood supply of the patient is life saving. She had immediate amputation of all three limbs and was transferred to the Intensive Care Unit. She never turned a hair and was out of ICU in three days and on the ward. Shortly after that she was transferred to the Rehabilitation Hospital. Her husband and children were incredibly supportive. After her transfer to rehab, I lost track of her. About a year or so later I was visiting my mother-in-law in a personal care facility with the pianist and we were having lunch in the dining room. A beautiful woman in an electric wheel chair came over to me with her husband and thanked me for looking after her. She was vibrant and her eyes sparkled. She was all there! Her life had resumed! Where does the power come from? Where is the Well that we can draw the strength from to continue to live a real life that is beyond simply existing? We didn't talk about faith that day, but I saw serenity. The Well that we draw from may be beyond definition for some, or defined by the curious faithful, but whatever it is, it is real!

Vaillaume Cello

I have no background knowledge of music or musical instruments since I am a surgical mug and tone deaf, but I am married to the pianist so I glean her periodic droppings. I go to the occasional musical soiree and nod at expressions of ecstasy shown by friends, so as to join in, but I know where I really belong and it's in the other kind of theatre: the operating theatre. I have tried! The pianist's mother was a concert cellist, and she played until she was eighty-five, and practiced in our home rather than her apartment since she was driving her adjacent apartment dwellers crazy with her unending scales! I was working one day years ago in the operating room with a colleague doing a long case and he was going on at the time, endlessly it seemed, about a side occupation that he did in addition to his general practice. He was a classical music lover and scholar and had an interest in brokering string instruments! He was enthusiastic about a Stradivarius that he had acquired the rights to, and had traveled to Olympic City, "Where the money is," he said, "to show it to a client." I idly listened to him as he rattled on gaily about his forays into the precious instrument trade, while I kept track at the same time of the surgical matter at hand. Then he said, "I have a bid on a Vaillaume cello as well. They are very rare but there is a client of mine who is in the market if I can find one. There is a beautiful one in Olympic city I can't access." "Oh yah!" I said, half listening, "We have one of those in our closet at home." There was silence. He knew I was a barbarian and couldn't tell the difference between a cello and a kettledrum. At least that's what he thought. "No!" he said. "Yes," I said, "I think it's in a closet somewhere." Well, there was no way that he wasn't going to see it that night. He said nothing more and assiduously paid attention to what we were doing to his patient for the balance of the case. Then, I couldn't hold him back. He bounded up the stairs at our home at 10 pm and said in an air of profound disbelief to the pianist, "You don't have a Vaillaume cello in your closet, do you?" "Yes", she said, "my mother bought it in Paris in 1928." My friend examined it carefully and then looked at me as if I were a newly hatched giant of the music industry. I felt like a poseur, but after all that talk, I wasn't going to let him know that I was just a surgical mug who knew what was in the closet.

Dirty Fingernails

Years ago, when I started doing orthopedic surgery in Winnipeg, newly hatched at the time, I remember sitting across at lunch from a very prominent internist, a stellar academic from a noted Winnipeg family. He was consulting that day and I was taken aback at what I thought were his dirty fingernails! As I think back now, I can't really remember that much about him, but the first image that always comes to mind is his fingernails. What an unworthy thought! However, what goes around comes around. I had not, at that time, heard of gardener's pigment. If one toils in the soil to any extent the fingernails will always seem dirty; there will be scabs and sores around your hands and calluses in palmar areas. If one is pinching, stopping, pricking or fine weeding one will have stains as well. Certainly, pruning vegetables will leave stains that challenge the scrub brush. Nails will be cracked and uneven! It has always been a challenge for me to metamorphose from grub to social butterfly in a single day. Don't tell me to wear gloves. No fine garden or potting work can be done with gloves. They are a refuge for the dilettante! I had a physician that scrubbed with me one day every fortnight for several years. He and I enjoyed gardening conversations when we scrubbed. He said to me how much he enjoyed working with me every second week. I was flattered that he appeared to compliment my skill, for which I erroneously thought he was in admiration. "Yes", he said, "The work allows me to get my fingernails really clean every fortnight." Ha! Trumped by the scrub sink. At least I was of some service to him. When I was working at surgery it took me half an hour scraping and bristling before a scrub to get my fingernails clean. Now that I'm retired there is no letup because in addition to "cleanliness is next to Godliness", which by the way is not true, there is still the job of serving communion as a lay congregant to 100 odd communicants, all of whom are taking clear sight of my fingernails. There is no respite! My legacy in the future: "Do you remember the name of that old fellow that served communion with gardener's pigment on his fingers?"

On Call Surgeon

Possibly the last time my younger colleagues in Orthopedics allowed me to take weekend calls was in the early '90s! That was also possibly the last time the pianist allowed me to cook for myself! I thought of this today when I looked at all the vitiligo on my right thumb. It was a beautiful weekend in the '90s and the Orthopedic colleagues were all away. The pianist was at Lotus Island potting, and I was in Lotus City, meeting the osseous needs of the populace! It was a quiet on-call that Friday evening at 8 o'clock or so and I thought I would make some popcorn while watching TV. As I began by heating my oil in a saucepan on the electric range, the phone rang from the Emergency with a problem. As I discussed the matter with the Emergency Room Physician for a while, there was a flash from the kitchen and my oil was on fire and shooting up to the ceiling. I raced in and grabbed the saucepan with the flaming oil and burned my thumb, so laid the saucepan in haste on the linoleum of the kitchen floor, which proceeded to burn as well as my thumb. The thumb developed a monster blister on the palmar aspect, and the linoleum, a large black melted welt in the center of the kitchen. I did the weekend call at that time, but kept a glove on regularly to contain the swelling and some of the blistering of the thumb. The hospital staff were impressed at how tough I was and also how stupid. I got through several surgical cases. My landlord at the apartment was gracious, and said, "It is time we redid that kitchen anyway!" Serendipity struck: I got out of taking weekend calls any further, obtained a kitchen renovation, reaffirmed that I needed feeding, and provided generalized merriment at the hospital! How can they say I wasn't useful?

A Surgeon Songster

Years ago, a noted senior surgeon in Lotus City often sang during his surgical procedure as he toiled away, freeing up the gall bladder, or small bowel, or whatever. He appeared to only know one tune and sang, or hummed it softly, but audibly. I think it relaxed him in his work and he was often unaware that he was singing, but sometimes he would catch himself, look fixedly at his scrub, and sing sotto voce as if he was always in command of himself. A co-conspirator admitting his scrub to the mysteries of his song. He usually had a commanding presence and could fix you with his eye and say something like, "Fresh fish," and you would ponder that a monumental message had been delivered, since he gave his phrases a certain sonority! Though singing is not that uncommon in routine surgical procedures, it is usually during the closure and when the mood lightens! Most surgeons that sing have a very modest repertoire to draw on and will drone on tonelessly, but it is relaxing to the surgical staff to know that the operator is at least content with the progress of his case! The senior one of whom I speak, however, only knew 'Nearer My God to Thee,' which would emerge at intervals during the procedure, not always at the most relaxed or routine part of the operation. Thankfully, the patients in those days were nearly always asleep, so they would not take the hymn as premonitory of some trip that they were not quite ready to take. On the other hand, the more optimistic of the patients may well have considered that they were simply being operated on by a saintly man, whose connection with God was immediate and proximate. Since, however, they lay blissfully ignorant of the heavenly melody that was mercilessly massacred by the operator, they could be reassured that their organ, which he had in his hands, was treated with more skill and care than any organ with which he may have attempted to accompany his hymn!

Operating Room Nurse

The nursing bureaucracy at the Lotus City hospital, where I toiled in Orthopedic surgery, decided, in their wisdom, to improve on what was working too well with the operating room charge nurses. Said to be in the interest of broadening the focus and utility of senior nurses for more flexible service usage, they concluded charge nurses should move from time to time to different services within the operating room. Senior nurses have a short learning curve, so they get up to speed quickly, but the decision never really took any of the surgeon's opinions into account. By that time, of course, in the corporate structure, it was none of our business despite the long established relationships we had developed with the charge nurses and the sort of seamlessness we had in the provision of patient care. The generals and colonels often hatch new ideas that break a few eggs on the corporal's plates. It is getting harder and harder to decide what rank is the more expendable, as our hands on people start to think about it. The curious thing is, as far as I know, I was the only one to raise an objection to this lateral move. Maybe it was because we had a treasure in our Orthopedic Service, but it was also fear for myself since I was getting older and as I was distracted when conversing from time to time with all and sundry, she would remind me what I should be doing. It was apparent that the bureaucracy would ignore any plea from me on this basis, particularly since all the other Service Chiefs lusted after my treasure. Like Menalaus, allowing Paris to steal and harbour Helen away, but unlike him, I had no wind left in my sail to get to Troy and steal her back. Since I was old and feeble, I had to resort to shock and awe and good humor to succeed. I therefore wrote to the nurse bureaucrats a simple letter of protest to say that I would kill myself if they moved Ms SL. They possibly had never received such a missive before, so, nonplussed, they relented in my case for a decent period of time. Perhaps they thought me mad and therefore concluded I needed a steady hand at the tiller. However, as the ship of state sailed on, she eventually left to take charge of the General Surgeons and I had to become a big boy again in the face of that delayed pillage.

The Advertiser

In the 1960s, the College of Physicians and Surgeons of BC forbade us from advertising for patients or making public claims of special skills. They were strict regulators! Claims of this nature were subject to sanctions by the Colleges! The newly arrived consultant was simply to modestly display their practice skill and knowledge to colleagues by their actions with their patients over the course of time and thereby gain a reputation for excellence or otherwise. Advertising is not forbidden now by the Colleges, but it is still frowned on as a low form of activity, smacking of commercialism and eschewing dignity. The new specialist in town in the '60s was required to simply hang a modest shingle and a tiny and dignified announcement of arrival in the paper (three times I think), and then wait until the colleagues saw fit to refer a surgical case. The growth of the surgical practice occurred ostensibly through practicing the three A's, Available, Affable and Able. That does not include Advertising! Remember of course that this was before Medicare and the few paying or insured patients were guardedly counseled by their General Practitioners. When the pianist and I moved to Lotus City with our little family in 1965 to start a surgical practice, I took a job at the Veterans Hospital to keep the wolf from the door while the slow process of developing a consulting practice began by establishing the confidence of the referring doctors. A tough old veteran had been having serious trouble with an old gunshot wound to the lower leg with bullet fragments and periodic septic drainage. He needed a below-knee amputation and the Veteran's Hospital Prosthetics Department was keen to try a new prosthetic technique with the immediate application of the artificial limb in the operating room and they talked me into giving it a try. The surgery went well. I was astounded to read a front page article in the Lotus City paper two or three days later relating an interview with my tough old patient who was walking around in the veteran's canteen, bearing full weight on the limb, extolling my surgical virtues! He was so elated he had phoned the paper! It wasn't very long before I was called to the mat by the College of Physicians and Surgeons for unfairly advertising! Several of my surgical confreres had complained and the Registrar of the College warned me that I was on thin ice. I pled innocence! However, Ha Ha,—it was a good start!

Phantom Limb

When a leg has been removed, for any reason, the image of the leg remains as a phantom and you may alight from your bed after a sound sleep and attempt to stand on something that is not there. The cortical imprint of your leg in the brain remains for some period of time despite the sensory input of something that no longer exists. This is called the phantom image. The larger map representation of neural areas in the brain for the lower limb are the joints, knee, ankle and the great toe. These are the phantom images identified most commonly by the patient, but as the brain adapts to the loss of limb, recognition occurs that there is a foreshortening of the phantom towards the stump end, rather than just fading away. Before it fades the foot may be felt on the end of the stump. If a history of severe chronic pain has been present for some time in the affected limb before amputation, then rather than just a phantom image alone, phantom pain will sometimes ensue. The brain we now know has a self adjusting ability to add or delete mapped areas that serve the body as needed and it is increasingly understood, but change is slower and less deliberate than we might wish, nevertheless the brain has remarkable potential to adapt in time. Where chronic pain has been present it is probable that the cortical representation is larger and adapts more slowly. Given this mystery of pain, or image, where the limb source no longer exists, it should follow that pain in other parts of the human vessel we call our own could still be remembered despite all manner of conditions that were present and now no longer show any discernible problem of pathology. Phantom pain in the back, gallbladder, shoulder disorders or a legion of other painful conditions that defy explanation are not entirely dissimilar in concept to phantom pain following limb amputation which is clinically unquestioned even if still ill understood. When they said in that scheme of things, that it's all in your head, it would have a different meaning if the analogy to phantom limb is a viable theory. Then it might mean, it's still on your cerebral cortex for a while and wait till the three pounds of grey matter remaps itself. It may be my simpleton's theory for a high powered neurophysiologist, but I am long in the tooth and too short of time to shut up.

The Surgical Scrub

In the usual course of events the referring family doctor would, from time to time, attend the surgical procedure for their patient and assist with the surgery out of interest for the patient's care and the informed knowledge that was to be gained for the patient's after care. This was certainly a desirable and attentive act to provide informed counsel to the family and longitudinal care for the patient. On the other hand, some family practitioners worked on a part time basis as professional surgical assistants when the patient's doctor was not available. Many of these doctors became very skilled and knowledgeable with respect to surgical techniques and their experience was enhanced since they assisted a wide variety of surgeons and absorbed the diverse skill sets that they observed. Every two weeks or so, a physician who was a long-standing surgical assistant helped me during one of my surgical days. We got on well and since we had a rather intense common interest in gardening it was often a topic we talked on about. We were standing at the scrub sink for the first case of the day one morning and he was particularly effusive in respect to his enjoyment of surgery and especially singled me out as a source of this delight. I must say that I was touched by his enthusiasm and my role in it. As we stood at the sink and talked of gardening, scrubbing our hands vigorously, cleaning our nails scrupulously, lathering hands and arms and wrists with the antiseptic soap, rinsing with copious amounts of water, we talked and time stood still. Basking in the glow of his approbation of what I thought referred to my surgical skill, he said, "Yes, I particularly like working with you because we scrub so completely and talk so long at the scrub sink that my gardening hands stay clean for my patients for days on end. That's why I enjoy coming with you every two weeks." He smiled at me with simple joy!

Thumb and Sinew

Ten days ago I ruptured my left thumb extensor tendon. Homo sapiens could never have spanned the head of Neanderthal man in order to bash it against a rock unless he could fully extend the thumb to reach an octave span. I have Rheumatoid arthritis and the tendon rupture was an attrition rupture due to the long standing tenosynovitis(inflammation), in the tunnel the tendon had to traverse in order to connect to its muscle, Extensor Pollicus Longus. It's not likely that at this stage of my life I will have to bash any heads against rocks, but I was still grateful for an early surgical repair. Because of the shoals, cobblestones and pitfalls of the four inches of Rheumatoid tenosynovitis at the wrist level, instead of gliding smoothly on a sea of serenity the tendon was secondarily softened and degenerate and liable to fray and split with little or no direct violence. A little like an angled mooring line chafed by a rough and blistered chock, rupturing suddenly with a little strain. There was no pain; I just suddenly noted after lawn cutting I could not move the thumb out from my palm. Luckily, we have been provided with two extensor tendons to the adjacent index finger. We only need one tendon, so a transfer of one of these tendons to replace the gap in the thumb tendon was done along with the removal of the erosive source. Now the index finger extensor muscle, Extensor Indices Proprius, and its tendon, will have to be taught to be a good little thumb extensor. Homo sapiens could never have developed fine and complex pinch unless they could lift the thumb out of the palm. Mankind's opposable thumb and complex digital sinews, brought into play by extension of the thumb is the singularity that has allowed the use of this early gift as the foundation for the development of intellect! The sinews are the source of mankind's strength, and dexterity! Very possibly Homo sapiens overcame Neanderthal man primarily due to the ability to perform better complex hand work from an opposable thumb that allowed fine pinch and grip and the intellect which ensued that led to clever deception as a result, rather than crude head bashing from the finger-thumb span alone. Intellect builds capacity, but capacity also builds intellect! There is a chicken and egg dilemma here. The march of the primates! We no longer have a hand that can only hook and clench like the arboreals; it can also grip and pinch: the mark of the terrestrials.

GARDENING

Maple Pole Bean Mania

Cobble Hill Ruthie and I were talking bean stakes yesterday as she was having trouble finding suitable ones. Her pole beans are now up! I told her I used fresh cut maple sapling shoots. They grow all over Lotus Island on the edge of the roadside ditches and are now 8 to 12 feet long! They are perfect for that use and they are free! If one is careful while cutting the shoot at the base so as to not disturb the cambium layer at the cut, then when one uses a dibble to make the holes to anchor the saplings, they will root at the buried node since they have the Force Majeure protected. One must have planted a node with the germinal root cells well below the surface of the dirt. When the shoots are first selected and cut while in the ditch, one may seem a madman to the vehicular traffic as they whiz by on the road at my eye-level. By spring, the shoots are branching in the ditch from all the nodes so they are trimmed to an inch on each sapling for the subsequent purchase of the bean stringers as they grow. The pole beans I use are Blue Lake, for no good reason other than I always have. These plants are heavy but they have strong positive thigmotropism and could cling to a pig-greased pole; nevertheless it is best to augment the support with the one inch branch purchase points which will help them to curl tightly and hang on. A good home-made dibble is an old broom. Drill a big hole 6 inches from the end of the handle and shove in a long bolt of matching size through the hole. Leave the worn out broom on as a lever. Your foot on the bolt plunges the dibble into the dirt and if you use the broom as a lever, you can wiggle your dibble. Stack the maple shoots around your bean sprouts and bind them together high up like a teepee. There are a lot of pluses to these maple stakes. As the stakes begin to root, the beans begin to climb with considerable celerity. The weight of the beans causes the flexible cane to bend, which tightens the bean stringers. The lateral stringers tighten too, so the bean-sapling unit becomes a taut one and therefore strong. The rooting capacity from both bean and sapling roots provide a firm founda-tion. The rooted maple sapling sucks up nitrogen but the bean is a nitrogen fixer and so, pays it forward. Isn't Mother Nature wonderful in its symbiosis? Success in human nature can take a lesson from the bean-stake unit. Strong; flexible; rooted; teamwork; paying forward; bean counting; and self-sustaining. Bean pods standing at your head height, where the air is clear and the sun is bright. As I thought about Ruthie yesterday, I also thought about Jack and his mother and his cow-for-bean enterprise. I have an interest in plant sounds, especially beans. Listen closely with each ear! Batteries charged so one can hear! Trill but soft, a little thrum! Fee and Fie, Foe and Fum!

Lotus Island Spring

March 17th: I was buzzed by the bumblebee today! As well, the pianist and I counted 14 Harbour seals clustered together; four lazy swimmers circling about and ten stationary swimmers treading or what goes for treading vertically in the water, sharp little snouts looking skyward; all waiting for the spawning herring to appear! The Indian Plum is in full flower and the Alder catkins are a cloud of red-brown. The Bufflehead ducks are weaving in and out of the cluster of waiting seals, taking their share of the small minnows the seals ignore. The raspberries and loganberries have started to leaf and the rhubarb is poking up through the leaf mold. The gooseberries and black currants are leafing out but the red currants are a little behind. The apples don't have any green on the leaf buds yet, but the pear's flower buds are swollen. The late storm surges over the last few days have thrown up an abundance of seaweed and have sucked out a lot of loose winter vegetation from the shore shrubs. This detritus has mixed together and harbours all the tiny denizens of the shore that feed the gulls and crows. The ground is like a wet sponge with all the rain, and the moss is especially thick this spring, giving a yellow-green luminosity to the canvas of Mother Nature, lying supine before us in the sunlight. I saw the little red squirrel today scampering about and he, (or she), allowed me to approach within four to five feet, which is pretty good. They are quick, but I worry because the eagles are starting on the hunt in earnest, feeding bigger fledglings! There is green, green, green everywhere on Lotus Island today and since St Patrick was of the green, it seems right. We haven't been diverted yet from the green by the vibrant colors that will come in abundance in another month. Even the daffodil blooms are still in the anteroom. The greens are restful and as holy as St. Patrick! A serene sort of vibrant. I think I'll toast the green with a Black Bush now!

Formication and Slug Fest

The tent caterpillars are now dropping like rain from their webs after the feeding frenzy, having denuded most of the soft leaf trees on Lotus Island. They are now resting for two weeks on any object they fall on, including the unwary. As they fall on the neck or head or clothing of the passerby they perform jactitations, swiveling and squirming here and there, giving rise to sensations of formication that linger in one's mind into the night when one wakes with the distinct, but erroneous sense, that something is still crawling on the neck, limb and trunk. Imagine the bizarre tactile hallucinations of the psychiatric patient afflicted with symptoms of formication and their desperation to sweep or swat what is not there. The orchardist, working in the tattered remains of his apple orchard amidst the insect drizzle dropping on him has this phenomenon to look forward to as he sleeps fitfully through the night. Soon, the worms that survive will cocoon 'til the middle of July and then emerge in force as yellow brown moths. The rain forest of Lotus Island has also bred a profusion of slugs this year; they munch the vegetation below in concert with the caterpillars munching the vegetation from above. I wondered if somehow they decided to work in cahoots. This ground feeding is especially vexing to the gardener of iris and dahlia. However, the early morning and nightly visits to the garden by the gardener, who must divide the slugs in half with sharp secateurs as he weaves his way through the rain of caterpillars, umbrella in one hand and secateurs in the other, is engaged in the most humane and satisfying of pursuits. Chopping and squashing the small bodies of the slugs and caterpillars that ooze out the green juices of the gardener's vegetation is sweet revenge but humane and instant death. Tossing at night in bed, waking in a dream world of squirm and slime is their revenge! It is war! Discard restraint! Carpe diem!

Shed Seaweed

My son-in-law and I were sitting on a beach log this afternoon and the tide was coming in with a strong onshore wind and moderate wave action in the harbor. For the past two weeks, there has been a large accumulation of shed sea lettuce and sundry other seaweed carried in by the tidal action. There is a lot of lateral tide movement on our beach as well, and the accessible part of the beach that welcomes and retains the weed is about five hundred feet long. After a few days, as the high tide lowers, the weed tossed up on the beach dries and loses some of its salinity and its definition. In the olden days, I used to collect much of this material for compost and top dressing. The ocean gives up its sea lettuce in August and its eelgrass in October, both of them gifted to those who scavenge the shore for that kind of treasure. I have always had a fantasy that if I had a donkey hitched to a large two-wheel cart I could walk the shore and pitchfork the drying weed into my cart with a lot more ease than trying to haul it up my 12 steps from the beach in a garbage pail. In the distant past, my Irish ancestors used this gift of seaweed to create soil on barren stoney headlands. It was where they were banished to from the fertile valley lands that were usurped from them. As we sat together on the log and looked reflectively at the drying weed, I thought aloud, "The line of drying weed above the tidemark is evenly ten feet wide now. Over the five hundred foot length it averages two inches thick! By my calculation that is 833.3 cubic feet of loose compost from that little area." What the sea gives up today it will take back tomorrow unless we act! I wish I had another lifespan where my fantasy was reality and I had a donkey and cart like my headland ancestors!

Dormant Spray

Luckily, we are beginning February with six sunny days in a row on the wet coast at Lotus Island. It is warm and dry enough, and that's what counts for spraying fruit trees. Light wind has meant that the sulfur and oil will not blow back in my face as much as usual, but still, you can't spray with the hose sprayer without some personal drenching. My glasses get repeatedly covered with oil and sulfur so I feel a little like, and look like Mr. Magoo, fumbling his way around the trees. In the past I had to climb my 12-foot fruit ladder to spray, because my hose pressure then was much less, and the oil on the slippery ladder made the job even more interesting. I wear a mask, so my glasses fog up from the inside as well from heavy breathing and it's hard to clean your spectacles, front and back, with slippery, oily, yellow-orange hands. At least I'm not 12 feet up the ladder now. I always remember with terror a patient of mine whose foot and leg slipped in between the oily rungs of the ladder and he turned upside down, fracturing his femur and remained suspended by the broken leg trapped inside the ladder, hollering bloody murder! A cautionary tale! I didn't dormant spray last winter, and it was much to my dismay when I saw the number of tent caterpillars and egg cases later that year and recalled the scabby pears and apples and the powdery mildew in the summer. Sulfur for the fungus and oil for the worms. In a sense, it is not unlike the preventative practice of medicine! I also see a lot of black and green algae on the wooden deck that is particularly thick and on the cement aggregate patio as well! There appears to be no end of things that I can squirt. I will also spray these areas with anti-fungus and algae compounds and then power wash. There is fungus, moss and lichen on the roof shingles too, though they are not so bad. Spraying the shady side of the roof is also on the agenda before it rains again. What a battle with Mother Nature this week, but I am girded for it and the only downside is a monster orange ring around the bathtub every night, regular change of one's yellow underwear and plenty of soap to get rid of the grease. If you choose to live in the rain forest, expect guests: Rain, Warmth, Pests, el Nino and the Friends of Rot! I can say without fear of contradiction that there is a tide in the affairs of men that making hay when the sun shines is seizing the day!

The Un-heavenly Host

And there came to Lotus Island in the year of the Dragon, the un-heavenly host, Malacosoma, the Western tent caterpillars, targeting and ravaging the soft leaf trees, devastating the landscape throughout the island. I am reminded of my drought years of the 40's, as a little boy on the bald prairie in southwestern Saskatchewan, with the grasshopper clouds eating every grain and leaf in sight, leaving so much bodily debris and grasshopper juice on the grill and windows of the Model A that it was difficult to travel. They even constructed grasshopper screens for the grill in those days. The windshields looked like a deluge of tobacco spit from the spittoon. The repeat worm plague that came on Lotus Island in a way resembled the plague of locusts in old Egypt and Kindersley from yester-millennium and yesteryear. The tent caterpillars on Lotus Island have now left the trees, since it is June and they are in cocoons, to undergo metamorphosis into the adult moth form in mid-July. There is, I am happy to report, a glimmer of light on the horizon, at least on the patch of ground of the pianist and the elderly eclectic gentleman. I took apart and examined 50 cocoons on my blueberry patch. The cocoons are of an intricate construction. They comprise an inner sack that contains the headless black nymph, awaiting transformation from Cinderella to Princess. This cocoon is a secondary oval silken sack, finely woven and close-ended. The outer cocoon is a loosely woven primary sack designed and spun initially by the worm to secure the later, finely spun inner sack to the leaf and branch. I investigated fifty compound sacks yesterday. There were only 5 sacks containing a healthy, black, headless nymph that would transform to a moth. The balance of the sacks, (45), contained dead or immature nymphs in a state of dissolution, empty sacks without exit holes, or parasitic larvae, not identified, foraging on nymph carcases. There were no gestating nymphs in a state of advanced metamorphosis. Today I see the devastated trees are beginning to re-leaf and the meagre 10 percent cycle survival of nymphs suggested by my admittedly short and local series still gives me some cause for optimism that the plague cycle has peaked. I may be dreaming in vain, but unlike Joseph of the multicolored coat, I cannot interpret a dream. I can only hope. Nevertheless, I am heartened to remember that when Pandora's amphora. was opened, we know that Hope still remained available in the jar, while the 10,000 Evils spread their wings and flew out into the world.

Tent Caterpillar Egg Cases

The tree pruner came the first week of January and did a nice job of the apple trees, pears and the Dolgo crab while listening to music through his earphones. He does the big trees, which are standards, and I do the smaller trees as I am now forbidden by my family to climb up my 12-foot fruit tree ladder. About 8 to 10 percent of the one and two year growth on the apple trees have tent caterpillar egg cases this winter. I think we all knew then that an infestation was going to happen this coming summer since the moths, Malacosoma, were extensive in the past summer on Lotus Island. We are yet to have a sharp frost, which I am still hoping will do some pest destruction. Rigorous pruning will get rid of a lot of the egg cases. Dormant oil sprays will deal with some of the egg cases that are left as well, since the eggs need air. Brian Minter has recommended three winter dormant sprays, but I struggle to complete one or two. The pear trees are safe because the leaves have a harder finish so the moths avoid egg-laying on pears. These caterpillars may be somewhat controlled on my apple trees with this shotgun approach, but the alders, birches, ocean spray, Rosa vulgaris and wild cherries are also loaded with egg cases and I can't prune the whole countryside, so in the end, we are going to have to rely on Mother Nature and the organic spray BT to interrupt the cycle along with the Tachinid wasp. Though I have never tried BT before, I am going to do so this spring. The trouble with BT is the larvae hatch in graduated stages, stepwise over six weeks here, so multiple sprays are needed. The pruner is a nice guy, but leaves his cuttings for me to pick up for shredding or burning. Thank goodness I've help, who does the bending and hauling while I do the shredding and burn what I can't shred on the beach. Shredding I am sure will destroy the egg cases when I compost the chips. Burning will certainly do it! Pruning, hauling, shredding, composting, burning and spraying, spraying and spraying. It's probably no more cost than a good gym membership and relatively as useful for fitness, played to a different rhythm.

Tent Caterpillar Moths

On Lotus Island the massive hatch of tent caterpillar moths has happened this week, the second week in July. They are everywhere, resting on the house siding and windows in hordes. Heat seekers invading every cranny and nook where a little more warmth and light can be found. This spring was a moderately bad year for the caterpillar tents on the apples, and other soft leaf trees so the moth invasion portends a much bigger year next year. Interestingly, I had made a search the past winter for egg cases and found few, so concluded that I didn't need to dormant spray. Big mistake! The trouble with Lotus Island is the "green movement" is so driven that even dormant spray is considered by many as dirty pool. This spring I spent a long time cutting off all the tents on my trees and drowning the tenters in the harbour, but I can't spare the time to drown the whole island population of caterpillars. Now we have to await the natural control mechanism by parasitic wasps. The tent caterpillars this spring, when observed, did not have that telltale white spot, dorsally, just behind their head. I should say the satisfying white spot. The parasitic wasp lays its egg there and on hatching the wasp larvae feed on the caterpillars. The rise of the worm population provokes a rise in the wasp population. Since the wasp larva has a specific need for that sort of food, as the tent caterpillar population declines, the wasp population eventually follows suit. Isn't Mother Nature grand? In the meantime, look next year for denuded spring time trees on the island due to the hatch of the massive number of egg cases that will come this fall and winter over. Fortunately Mother Nature provides a secondary leaf recovery. If you have apples, plums and cherries, prepare for the worst! The tree can survive well without fruit, but not without the energy produced by abundant leaves. Mother Nature is both grand and wise and looks down the road!

Scatological Investigations

The varied and colourful droppings of the ubiquitous North Western Crow are a useful source of information about the eclectic nature of their dietary habits. For those of us with a scatological bent, the seasonal changes and omnivorous habits of this species, Corvus caurinus, are worthy of outlet study since they are one of the most adaptable of birds, their success based on diet and opportunism. The pianist and I, living as we do in the country on Lotus Island, have the fortune, or misfortune, of having a large painted deck under three mature Western Red Cedar trees that serve as a table-toilet for crows. The volume and character of the droppings change remarkably through the season from both tree and anus. As I clear the tree droppings on the deck and its furniture daily, with my gas powered blower, I observe dry small cones, lichen and moss fragments arising somewhat from the crows' disturbance and the little red squirrel scratchings, and the seasonal needle drop. In the spring, small dead cedar branches are ripped from the tree by crows for nest repair and are often dropped, or dismissed for being unsuitable for repair. When I have rid the deck of tree detritus, I then have the opportunity to investigate the associated scat and sticky food leftovers, clam shells, half eaten cherries and red plums that have slipped through their toes after initially being pinioned on the branch. Naked cherry and plum stones, flesh successfully eaten in full; the scat from a diet of clams and tube worms, small birds or baby quail, sweet cherries and wild plums, pear and apple fragments; all leave a digested, colourful deposit; brown and crunchy, smooth or particulate, black and punctate, white and thin and watery; all with interesting textural variety and compelling graphic intricacies within the scat splat; Rorschach-like in nature: all scat pockmarking the deck with remarkable tenacity, resistant even to the gas powered hose sprayer and requiring a stiff brush, elbow grease and spray to remove. Even the glass-topped table and patio chairs are a scat target and all varieties are equally adherent on the glass and metal. If you are willing to pay the price for clean, pristine, aseptic eating on a deck, under spreading cedar trees, in crow and berry territory, you will never resent the blow, spray and brush activity. Between the scat and the copious water spray, the cedars are second-ary beneficiaries for the role they serve as a table-toilet for our feathered friends. Live and let live with Mother Nature in all her glory.

Lilacs

While one can admire the dedication of the French hybridizers in the development and selection of superior cultivars of Lilacs, there is a homely side to the old timers of yesteryear and even more so, the Lilac progenitors. Syringia vulgaris may be seen in their varietal splendor at The Royal Botanical Garden in Hamilton Ontario as the pianist and I observed when we visited some years ago. They advertise, "The largest lilac collection in the world." Spouting off! Despite Island being Rhododendron country, Lilacs have a place everywhere as they are a ubiquitous presence. Every barn and abandoned house on the more sheltered prairies and the BC interiors had a hardy old timer, surviving after a fashion without demanding a great deal of care. Maybe not as varied and fancy as the new grafted cultivars, but a survivor to be admired, with a touch of class; colour and fragrance added to a sometimes drab environment. I have two lilacs that are grafted specimens and despite horror from the fanciers, I am withstanding the pressure from them by allowing a limited growth of the suckers alongside the cultivars! Though I treasure the cultivar, the progenitor is the creation of Mother Nature rather than the French hybridizer, and it reminds us where both we and the sucker developed from, and what we have become, for better or for worse. We should never forget our root stocks and it works best if we still remember and harbour them. It's like having grandpa up in a spare bedroom in the mansion of the starlet, where we can still see him getting by with his homely growth even on his thin gruel! The progenitor has small florets on spare heads, but it is history and if the shrub growth is contained by removing most of the suckers, but retaining one or two, as I did today, it provides some interest to those of us who are probably quirky and know down deep that "beauty is still in the eye of the beholder" and we don't have to hide grandpa from general view. If you don't remove most of the suckers they will overcome your cultivar because the progenitor has as vigorous vegetative growth as its maker, Mother Nature. There is no harm in recognizing and prizing our origins, thick or thin and tough as nails!

Grass is a plant

Sometimes it's hard to recall that grass is a plant when you see the beautifully cut carpet lawn of the North American golf course! The so-called lawn of the bucolic Lotus Island set is often the meadow grasses, cut to a higher measured level to retain, "uniformity!" Taming the meadow grasses into a simulated lawn does not allow one to discard the recognition that one's grasses are a plant. As I have previously mentioned, we have 200 varieties of grasses on the Pacific Northwest and they vary greatly in growth habit! They are not, on the whole, all genetically engineered to flourish at half an inch or less. Neatness doesn't count, but sensitivity does if the free spirits of Mother Nature are allowed to flourish! I'm not suggesting for one minute that the fairway be cut to impede the ball from rolling. I'm not even suggesting the lawn-proud urbanite change his ways if the genetics of the turf are such that a half-inch set is a healthy thing! It's just that the heterogeneous grasses of Mother Nature will live together in perfect accord if you raise the bar a lot as you cut your so-called lawn. The grasses have been living together for centuries along with a mix of plants within the lawn on Lotus Island without a lot of outside help. The plants within the lawn are sometimes mistaken for green weeds by outsiders. The dominance of the composition of the so-called lawn varies from time to time depending on the changes in the climate. Celebrate that! Monoculture as a general rule in most instances leads to less adaptable outcomes. Mother Nature is wise! Aristotle said, "Nature does nothing in vain." Aristotle was also wise. Bunnies and deer prefer mixed herbaceous food as well. Bunnies and deer are also wise. Celebrate that too! If we want to keep the ball rolling, then limit monoculture to golf and lawn bowling.

Gunnera Attacked

It's fall, and the bucks of the black tailed deer on Lotus Island, a subspecies of mule deer, are in rut! Whether they are getting rid of their antler velvet to get into fighting trim, or practicing their moves against upcoming adversaries, or both, is moot. Either way, the young bucks are preparing for the coming conflict. Once the testosterone arises in deer or man, more activity will take place from the mid-brain. Whatever harm did my Gunnera plants do to the bucks? And yet, it is a convenient foil to attack: an inert adversary like a punching bag. The stems of Gunnera are coarse with rough spinous projections, sufficiently sharp to remove the antler velvet! After that little favour by the plant, it's a short and unloving step to give the stems a good whacking with the newly hardened antlers. I've always said that Gunnera is a manly plant, so I suppose the deer feel it is a worthy opponent. The warrior class is simply doing what is necessary to perpetuate their species. Luckily for the gardener, the bucks are benign warriors throughout the growing year until fall, so the Gunnera enjoys a pristine existence until then. Actually, it is fortuitous that the rut begins in the fall, since it is nearly the end of the plant's season anyway, so it's a good way for the Gunnera to go out fighting. The plus for all this is that the bucks stop rubbing on the smaller ornamental trees which would otherwise be victimized. I hate the idea of surrounding all the little trees with wire cages. If you are not going to restrain the warrior class by fencing them out of your property, you must respect their need to train, but hope that they will restrain themselves by confining their battle happily to the Gunnera, acting as my serendipitous stalking horse! That said, one gives thanks that young and fearless males are not the equivalent of a walking gonad controlled by the midbrain throughout the year! Wreaking havoc unselectively! If rut and heat went throughout the year, the plant species would indeed be in jeopardy!

Penny for your Plots

On Monday, my daughters and their partners came and planted the ailing elderly gentleman's dahlias in his time-established (in modesty I can't say honored) protocol. In short, when the soil warms and the muck goes, a hole is dug every 18 inches, 8 inches deep; a handful of 13-16-10 is chucked in; the Mantis tiller is jumped from hole to hole to make a soft feathery bed for the root. The dahlia root is chucked in on its soft little prepared bed, right side up, and a 5 foot rebar is hammered in next to the creature on its north side so we know the shoot will emerge south of the rebar when we first weed. The bulb is covered with 2 inches of soil and lightly tamped. Later, the hole is hilled in as the sprouts grow and are gently tied to the rebar! My family planted over 200 dahlias in this exemplary fashion. One of the major faults of some large flowered exhibition dahlias is weak flower stems! Large blooms with weak stems and the resultant floppy, droopy appearance is a big no-no! Out with those bulbs in the fall! Off with their heads in the summer like the Queen of Hearts, no mercy. Some time ago the pianist noted that the cut bouquets of tulips she buys that droop become ramrod straight in the vase if a couple of copper pennies are placed in the water at the time of arrangement or later. I have, in the past, scoffed at her assertion, accusing her of swami-thinking and avoiding probability value reporting, but her repeated assessments in our living room, anecdotally suggests penny energy might be real. Unfortunately, I didn't think of pennies and her protocol in time to consider activating the technique into my current dahlia planting scheme. There is nothing to lose. I may hold off "out with the bulbs in the fall" for another year. I'll do penny for your plot next year if I am still here and lively. Another use for the dying Canadian penny! Chucking a few otherwise redundant pennies in the hole at the time of planting maybe a cure for weak stems of the more beautiful of the droopy dahlia varieties that are worth keeping, but without favorable p-values I'm not holding my breath. Note: if you really want to be bothered exhibiting your dahlias, plant them 3 feet apart, not 18 inches.

Winter Ducks

The Lotus Island harbour today, in early November, is teeming with American widgeons and bufflehead ducks! They come back to the same place in the harbour year after year and you could set your calendar on the day of their return. Vegetarians and carnivores! Dabbling ducks and diving ducks. They will be here all winter, sheltered in our little spot in the harbour to our great delight. The eagles have not returned yet to begin again with their connubial activity, so the ducks have a short reprieve from danger. The buffleheads are much smaller than the widgeons, so are easier for the eagles to carry to their fledglings. The widgeon crowd serenely together, float along, seemingly unhurried, occasionally dabbling down when close to shore for plant food. They don't need to hurry because the plants wait for them! Their pace is unruffled! Why wouldn't it be? They are the gatherer society. When they dabble down, their little feathered arses stick straight up in the air. The little buffleheads skitter along, wings flapping repeatedly, posturing and diving and darting hither and yon! You can always identify them by the wake they leave; they move so fast with both feet and wings going a mile a minute; in or on the water, chasing flesh! No wonder they are in a hurry. Their prey waits for no bufflehead so they have to be quick about it if they are to be a successful hunter society! The seagulls pester them, hoping they will drop the prey, but the buffleheads have an answer to that noisy and opportunistic feathered society. They swallow their prey under water where no seagull will go. Then they emerge after they dive, well away from the gulls. They spend much of their time swimming around and through the widgeon flock so they give the appearance of hare among the tortoises. Curiously, the only winter ducks we usually see now are these two species. In days of yore there were many winter species that visited but the varieties seem to have dried up. I don't know why. The harbour provides an abundant source of both plant and animal food-stuffs and the two species don't compete because of the nature of their respective diets. Aside from the eagles picking them off, their winter sojourn is untroubled!

For the pianist and me, we could watch them all day; so for us familiarity never breeds contempt!

Black Bamboo

In 1971 in Lotus City I combined several clumps of Black Bamboo (*Phyllostachys nigra*) along with Mexican Fan Palms and a tan-colored aggregate of a pebble like nature called Saturnalite. These materials were planted in a deep cleft in a rock hill. It appeared like a dry riverbed. Saturnalite is produced by heated and blown clay bodies to produce a popcorn-like dry aggregate. It was quite beautiful, light and easy to work with, but had no nourishment for the plants. They required circumscribed soil deposited under the Saturnalite at each plant station. I wanted the bamboo to remain clumped and it did. My information at the time was that Black Bamboo was of a naturally clumping nature and would not spread. Since there had been an embargo on bamboo at around that time and particularly Black Bamboo, I was pleased to have it, and I might have imagined I was in China as I sat, daydreaming on my dry riverbed. We moved from Lotus City to Lotus Island, both in the Pacific Northwest, much later and I took some rooted portions of the bamboo clumps with me. Lotus Island and Lotus City have moderate winter temperatures that are at the top of cold tolerance for Black Bamboo, so the plants appreciate shelter. They are still in my garden on Lotus Island today, protected from cold ocean winds by the mixed windbreak hedges of Mother Nature. The Black Bamboo plantings weathered a particularly cold winter in 2010 with some top foliage loss. In the garden here, they are in three big clumps, but this year they have started to move! They have, for the first time in 35 years, begun to develop spreading rhizomes in spades! The clumps are monstrous and have probably responded to now-exhausted soil by seeking fertile land, sending probing rhizomes and creating new plants at a distance. When the bamboo was growing in Lotus City in the dry riverbed there was no nourishment from Saturnalite, so I provided water and fertilizer to the limited soil ball they lived on. There was no initiative on their part to look further on their own. On the acreage of Lotus Island, even though clumping was their nature, they moved abroad, spreading and seeking new wealth when they had exhausted what they had for food in the old ground. Populations of anything, plant or animal, including human, do what they have to do, traveling to new ground, sacrificing their nature to survive and thrive. The alternatives are dependence, attrition, or death. It goes to show that the classification of clumping or spreading, in plant and animal, fails to account for the contingent capacity to change and move with whatever means is necessary to survive! Climate and food trump sticking in the mud, in the plant and animal world!

FOOD

A Food Source

Mother Nature and Human Nature are really One. If we see ourselves as a food source amongst our other useful attributes, we can embrace the universality of all the ions and atoms we are related to, plant and animal and mineral that spend much of the time eating and being eaten, digested, or absorbed by one another while perched on the food chain of life and death. If you believe that you are at the top of the food chain, know that you are living food for the mosquito, tape worm, E.coli, the commensals, and at the end, the Yew tree, the grass, the vultures, the carrion beetles and other members of the so-called lower orders that enjoy you in perpetuity, along with the maggots that eventually conquer the embalmer's gift. The so-called lower end of the food chain, for which we are a constant source of food, completes the circle of life. We eventually embrace and enter the mineral world when that erstwhile flesh and bone arises again in new vegetation. Therefore, it is hard to call any feeder the lower order, since we all are part of the wheel of life. There is no humiliation in this matter. There is no humiliation in being one with Human Nature and Mother Nature. The sin in the Garden of Eden was the sin of believing that we were different from the garden and could freely eat of the Tree of Knowledge, thinking we were of another substance from the tree, rather than be content in the shade of the Tree of Life!

Augmented KD

The pianist and I were at a dinner party last evening and, amidst other topics, food and drink were both consumed and a topic of conversation. Favorite foods and recipes, particularly pasta and the creative opportunities it enabled, gave the to and fro to a lively and entertaining discussion. The pianist was engaged in the conversation, but since my culinary skills and knowledge are limited, I contributed little of consequence. That is, until I mentioned that my favorite default meal was augmented KD. If the pianist was away and I was on my own, KD was the choice, with added sharp cheese and butter and cream. Gales of laughter! Oh well! At least my dignity was saved by my assurance that I always ate it from the plate, and the augmentation rendered it less shockingly orange and more comforting. Later, as I went to sleep that night, I thought of my friend and his addiction to KD. Years ago, my young colleague, who was a busy GP, split from his wife and, to save money, slept in his office and subsisted on a diet that was almost solely KD. His practice was immense, so time was of the essence for him, and his putative settlement, an expense that was looming, remained an additional worry of his. Six or eight months later he told me he was concerned that he may have leukemia, as he had recently noticed generalized bruising, his gums had started to bleed, he had limb pain consistent with subperiosteal hemorrhages and unaccountable weight loss was apparent. When he finally checked in from the investigations, he was somewhat relieved to be diagnosed with scurvy! KD is augmented by all sorts of good vitamins and minerals as well now, but not Vitamin C because it is heat labile. Adding chopped up wiener chunks to your KD will not avoid scurvy and won't even make it appear pretty. My advice is, stay married, drink orange juice with your KD if you are addicted, use KD sparingly, rather than as a regular default meal, and don't save time and effort by eating it out of the pot, at least for the sake of preserving your already diminished dignity!

Wheat grass

At the Lotus Island market every weekend, wheatgrass is sold as a healthful food when prepared as a juice, with nutritional and restorative powers. Its virtues seemed to me to be something of a more modern and innovative discovery, though it was investigated in the 30s and 40s, and the art of juicing and marketing the drink occurred in the 50s. Remarkable claims have been made as to its benefits. Fancy then, that Rabelais (1494 to 1553), physician, author and theologian, in his book about the adventures of Gargantua and Pantagruel (1534), described the benefits of "wheat in the blade." There is truly nothing new under the sun. I'm not sure Rabelais is everyone's cup of tea, but here goes. He writes, "From wheat in the blade you make a fine green sauce, simple to mix and easy to digest, which rejoices the brain, exhilarates the animal spirits, delights the sight, induces the appetite, pleases the taste, fortifies the heart, tickles the tongue, clarifies the complexion, strengthens the muscles, tempers the blood, eases the diaphragm, refreshes the liver, unblocks the spleen, comforts the kidneys, relaxes the vertebrae, empties the ureters, dilates the spermatic glands, tautens the testicle strings, purges the bladder, swells the genitals, straightens the foreskin, hardens the ballock, and rectifies the member: giving you a good belly, and good belching, farting-both noisy and silent- shitting, pissing, sneezing, crying, coughing, spitting, vomiting, yawning, snotting, breathing, inhaling, exhaling, snoring, sweating, and erections of the john-thomas: also countless other rare advantages." The observations of Rabelais render the modern pitch a bit pallid, wouldn't you agree?

Regal Gooseberry Jam

Today I picked four pounds of dead ripe gooseberries from my bush: not rosy red, but the deeper purple red colour of venous blood from a cyanosed patient! Picking gooseberries is hard work; avoiding the heavy thorns with a glove on the left hand to control the branch; picking selectively since the berries ripen to sweetness intermittently over a month. Even the dead ripe need a tug since the berries drop very late. I interim prune with the secateur as I pick, since the bush is huge and to get to its center without tearing your shirt or skin is the aim. Good pruning is necessary to get new wood to grow, as the berries are better on new wood than old. The gooseberry bush is next to a patch of red currants which I now leave on the bushes as a stalking horse for the birds since red currants act as a magnet and mine contain current maggot; protein for the birds. Mm mm good. Since the skin of the gooseberry is tough and the armed branches are formidable, the birds leave them alone for an easier target. I spent an hour or more after the pick today removing the occasional stem and the constantly present frass, (my term for the withered remains of the flower). This is a tedious task. The next step was to freeze them in Ziplock bags for jam preparation. The freezing allows the juices to run more freely with cooking and it requires less water to be added. At jamming time the berries are softened in the microwave with enough water to minimally cover them, and then they are mashed. Do not puree since the cooked berry skin is an essential feature of the jam. Sugar is added, equal parts, and cooked with the berry mash until the gel point or appropriate thickness approaches. If anyone thinks it is madness to go to all this work for a little jam, it is not. Gooseberry jam is a rare essence, not easily obtained and a high style of product, certainly ego-satisfying both to the purveyor and recipient. As it is with the essential essence of people of a regal nature, tough-skinned, singular and prickly as a gooseberry, it makes the work of those of us who choose to bring their sweetness and excellence to the fore much more satisfying, since we labour in order to please and soften their hauteur. I love white bread and gooseberry jam, but as sweet and piquant accompaniments to meat it has also been tested and toasted over the centuries. Crabapple and chicken: applesauce and pork: cranberry and turkey: mint and lamb: Montmorency cherries and game: but lapin and gooseberry: it rocks!

Quince Jelly

Two mature and knowledgeable ladies I know who like to make quince jelly took a large portion of my Quince crop this past month, but I still had a number of these fruits that I tried to get rid of, unsuccessfully. Quince jelly is not for everyone! The flavour is rather unique. It has, however, an aromatic quality and a great deal more character than its cousins, the apple and the pear, so I could not bring myself to discard the basket full of the fuzzy yellow fruit that was left behind after the ladies picked through them. I made my own quince jelly last week and it was very successful as the pectin content is high, even in the fully-ripened and over-ripened fruit that I used. Since quality jelly demands not only taste, but colour and gel quality, my product will rate highly for the scarce aficionado who appreciates the unusual and less readily acquainted flavour and appearance provided by quince jelly. The jelly in the jar has a colour of fine orange furniture oil, uniquely beautiful as well, to differentiate it from common red. I am also hoping that my value-added product will entice the extraordinarily wary who avoid the primary product, the fruit, but who could become a new enthusiast after trying the jelly. Those of low and undistinguished taste who require the more usual jellies on their toast can content themselves with the predictable. I do not intend to waste my time to proselytize any further to the un-adventuresome. You may think I am going overboard on this matter and if so, you are probably right as my position is not all that clean. I am one of the few on Lotus Island that has a fully productive Quince tree, (Cydonia oblonga) and pride and ego I confess, has entered its ugly head as it gives me, I suppose, somewhat meager and pathetic bragging rights. I have no shame! I am sure there are more elderly eclectic ladies on Lotus Island that can be enticed with my jelly, as I will allow it to speak for itself! As I was putting my jelly on the shelf, I heard a small sound from a jar. I listened carefully and think I heard it say, "Res ipsa loquitor, Oblonga thanks you."

Fondue and Artichokes

In the 60's, fondue was all the rage, at least in our neck of the woods! Slow eating was in! Cool folks huddled around hot cooking oil in a communal pot on the dining room table. Cubes of beef sizzling on a sharp fork, falling off of the fork into the pot; sometime-chefs fumbling around with the fork to find their cube and knocking off everyone else's meat in the process. The product, often crispy fried as a result of fumble frying was then dipped in creamy dill or plum sauce. Hauled across the table, pot to plate to mouth, dripping grease on the table and burning the mouth: clearly I was not fond of fondue, but the pianist liked it and also pursued chocolate fondue with strawberries and cheese fondue with bread cubes. For those who enjoyed a languid, more cognitive eating style, it could be a conversational bonanza while your little cube was cooking, your mouth empty and working overtime despite the constant attention to keeping the oil boiling, the meat from being over done and the gymnastics with the forks, plus deciding whose fork is whose. To achieve that languid space with fondue action going on, you just had to eat less. Fondue is not a guy thing, and I was driven more by the hypothalamus and the parotid gland to fill up fast, so mercifully for me, fondue has succumbed to time and the rat race! The garden at Lotus Island still has Globe Artichokes, another major contributor to the Slow Loris eating industry! Sucking and scraping away at the sepals of the flower bud after dipping in garlic butter, the eater will have to bath and change his clothing to rid the grease and fuzz. Dipping the soft and tasteless bases of the calyx requires a preemptive greasy act of slow dissection, ridding oneself of the nascent fuzzy petals which guarantees the rest of your meal will get cold while filling the garbage pail with the inedible 90 percent of the artichoke. My advice to artichoke lovers is let them flower into their magnificent purple thistle-like flower head and put them on the table as a table centre with your meat, ketchup and potatoes! Quelle delicatesse.

WORDS

When the Rubber Hits the Road

I have often read another person's written content publicly; poetry, short stories, Scripture passages, but have never read my own material to an audience till recently! It's easy to read another's material since there is no responsibility for content other than the choice of what to inflict on others! Material that has lasted the test of time, is well known, and classic, is rarely inflicted on anyone and even if you don't read that well, the material will carry you. Your own stuff is a different matter. Despite the fact that I may like my own work; I have convinced myself that I am writing for myself; that I feel my craft is adequate and the content authentic; there is still a need for approval, and to read it to an audience is daunting. We're human! One can write for money, or love, or to scorn, but if one really writes largely for oneself, it is therapy. One can write from one's mind, or heart, or soul, but no matter what one does write, it is biography. It always says something about us. When we write we can get it all out, purge, and spill the words in front of the public on a page. Confining yourself to putting your material on a page gives a comfortable distance to protect yourself. There is space of a sort and one can hide behind a page. It's another matter to read it to the public! That's when the rubber hits the road! Suddenly the distance between reader and writer is gone and they are one. Suddenly the distance between reader/writer and audience is gone! Suddenly all this brave and foolish bullshit about writing for oneself is gone. We stand bare-assed and prepared to be embarrassed. Courage! Those who write understand. They know about exposure. They know about empathy. They know about failure! If we speak to an audience of friends who write, all of us know we don't have to amount to anything to be loved. When this rubber hits friendly concrete like that it has a little more bounce to it.

Random Harvest

The top banana of the Greek Gods, mighty Zeus, swallowed his wife Metis at the time that she was pregnant with Athena. Eventually, Metis gave birth, and Athena, in utero at the time of the meal, had to emerge eventually, twice born, through the top of Zeus' head. This isn't a story about food or obstetrics or neurosurgery or even a cranky husband though it may brush some or all of these topics. It's about control, or rather the lack of it. Zeus had to deal with Athena's arrival on her timetable rather on one of his choosing. She ended up being useful to him, rather than stronger than him as he had originally feared! Segueing along, if I am a fermentation vat, from time to time a bubble arises from below, breaks my surface with a "boing," and produces a spreading ring that lasts a while. The vat doesn't know when the bubble is going to break out and can't stifle it. Like Athena, the bubble rises up in its own time, ruffles the surface, and thereby is part of the fermentation. The quality of the product will be up to the taste of the tasters. The random harvest of thoughts that arise de novo; grasped at and scribbled about, without questioning the timing of the birth process, and without stifling yourself, is therapy of a sort, like accepting a quizzical stroll through your head. It's clear that there is a lot to see there, but it only shows itself to you when it will. Like Zeus, I must have eaten a lot of stuff in my life that is still sitting around waiting to be born, or wanting to be born, but perhaps I am too thick-skulled yet to let it all out. Possibly I am still stuffed with stuff and long to empty myself, but I must wait for Athena, Goddess of Wisdom to emerge. It's at least intriguing to me what the muse will say next, and when the bubble will arise. Constipated notwithstanding, I am content to sit on the stoop and wait for it.

Casuistry

Casuistry may seem an obscure word, but it is a noun, functionally, but not literally more often employed in the world at the moment than any other I can think of, exemplifying all advertising, political rhetoric, advocacy groups and legal selectivity. It does not always use hyperbole. Worse! It is a subtler word, more damaging and employing both suckage and hyperbole as well as deceptive reasonableness. Vacuuming up what it wishes you to ignore and blowing on endlessly about what it wishes that you not ignore. It can be seen in newsprint and the Internet and in the clever constructions from the comment sections. It is more convincing to those who hear or read things, the spectators of life, than to those who do things. Unfortunately, there is such a limited breadth of things we can do, and such a wide breadth of things we can watch! The only object of the casuist is to convince! We must always ask what is in the interest of the convincer? The reaction of the audience may be cynical and believe nothing, or gullible and believe everything, or hopefully somewhere in between. Evidence used to be in the eye of the beholder and arguable but now, technology is so artful and casuistry so slippery that in beholding we often still can't tell where we are at. You may in fact have already become aware that this paragraph I have written is an example of casuistry. It may not rank as a clever construction, but it smacks of too much generalization to be on the high road. Still, it probably contains a tuppence worth of truth that those who already share the premise about unholy casuistry will find somewhat satisfying. If the file folder in your cerebral cortex is only available for A and not for B, then A will be accepted and B rejected. How do we get to a folder AB? I wish I knew!

Eg Latin

For years our family has spoken Eg Latin, a superior subset of Pig Latin that has much greater cypher advantage than some other forms of Pig Latin. Eg Latin is either not generally known, or alternatively it is below dignity for most of the linguistically superior amongst us! It was used in fun, a harmless preoccupation, but was completely confounding to the uninitiated. In the standard Pig Latin the post fix, AY, is placed at the end of the word behind the transposed first consonant or consonant cluster. Hence Rhinocerous would be hinocerousRay or perhaps inocerousRhay! Not too difficult to translate even for the usually easily confounded. In Eg Latin, each syllable is treated by EG following the consonant or its cluster, so Rhinocerous is transposed as Rheginegocegeregous! If there is no consonant, but a vowel leading the syllable, the Eg precedes, such as in "over", egoveger! You may think this is hard to become fluent in, but it is not! Small children will take to it like a duck to water! Start with simple stuff like Legategin! Like Pegig! It is much harder to write Eg Latin, than to verbalize! I was taught this foolishness by my father and have transferred it to the succeeding generations successfully. I remember flying with our family somewhere years ago and talking EG Latin quietly to a kid that was misbehaving, when the family behind us joined the conversation, much to our delight. I am completely illiterate in any language except English, so I scrape the bottom of the barrel as my only claim to linguistic pluralism is derived from the country of EG.

Dementia Defended

One of the early signs of dementia includes having to hunt for your own Easter eggs, which you laid the day before, and repeating yourself endlessly. Then, yesterday I laid a new egg by repeating the same context of a blog I had previously written; different words, but the same context, and then failed to recognize it until too late. That very thing occurred last night with "The Surgical Scrub" and recognition belatedly of an earlier post called "Dirty Fingernails." One might think that it's easy to avoid duplication when writing, but why should the written word be regarded any differently than the oral word, when repeated? I have often heard many people say, "Have I told you this before?" And they have, again and again! So what's the difference? If I write about the same thing again, I don't mind as long as the words are newly minted and it's not again and again and again. That's just me! I have listened to the same old jokes and stories from the same people I admire, told many times to the same other people for years. It's like fine old wine, or a story, gilded, not tarnished, with the patina of long life. Untold numbers of men prefer the clothing that they have worn for years rather than new ones, the only provision being that they still fit. Both words and clothing speak of us. My children, and I know most other children as well, prefer the enfolding grip of stories often told, rather than the newly told. The common refrain was, "No, not that one, tell us the one we always like!" When the pianist plays at the extended care home, the old familiars are the ones for them; "In the Garden," every week of the year. Why should oral always trump written, even though oral gets away with it because there is no record of repetition? For some inexplicable reason a subject might bear writing again with a new adjective or two, simply for the thrill of inadvertently revisiting one's creation and savouring it again, tasting your old Easter eggs anew. Maybe this old saw best applies for the very old and the very young.

Grammatical Corruption Redacted

Its, it's and 'tis! My colleague castigates me repeatedly for my misuse of "it's" for the possessive pronoun, which I must admit I am not careful about. However in "it's" and my defense, in an editing workshop last week I posed a question to the group by asking, "Why, if the apostrophe in a mule's ears are long and hairy, why not "it's" ears are long and hairy since the apostrophized it's is a substitute for mule and possessive is still possessive?" To say as we do now, that the possessive "its" ought not to have an apostrophe, while the noun it substitutes for does, makes no sense to me. The consensus at the workshop was that the apostrophe differentiated the usage of the two words, it's and its. Well, that's obvious, but why would anyone care to go there? The context of the sentence declares the meaning and usage well enough without mutilating the word! Then I read in the grammar detective, that "it's" as a possessive pronoun, was used on a regular basis a couple of centuries ago, but was changed to "its" when "'tis" became deemed archaic, so "it's" was substituted for "'tis" as a contraction of "it is" and so, "it's" was shoved out of the rightful place as a possessive by the rule of happy and meddlesome grammarians. I can hardly wait to confront the colleague with my newfound knowledge and, to me, picayune changes in the past that altered principle. We could start using "'tis" again, for "it is", and talk about mule's ears and it's hooves without a lame excuse about lack of differentiation. What a contrarian either I am, or English is! The argument though, will be a lost cause. Lots of English words have several meanings, never confused within the context of the sentence. If you think I am snowing you, expect flakes like me to fall on your word parade. Ah well, better switch than fight, so it's easier to fagaddaboudit!

Wordsmiths

Received clusters of designated symbols we call words can be either seen or heard. The 2nd cranial nerve, the optic nerve, will mediate the seen word to the occipital cortex. The heard word will be mediated by the auditory branch of the 8th cranial nerve to the cortical temporal lobe. These different entry points, and transfers to the imprinting areas inevitably lead to different perception despite the excellence of the subsequent processing and integrative activity of the brain. Maybe not, but Common Sense and Ockham's Razor are always of some value. The symbols you learned to see do not necessarily reflect the symbols you learned to hear before you could read. Since these symbols have become the stuff of communication, then oral and written language is the stuff of life. Many people have developed listening skills that commit much of what they hear to memory: the oral, an older and more primitive tradition. Others have highly refined visual skills and are visual learners, so reading and writing (seeing), leads to better retention. When we read to others we transport the visual symbols to the listener's ear. It will go from our imprinted symbols in the occipital cortex, to the spoken clusters, to the listener's ear, to their temporal lobe. The symbols will be filtered and compounded for the listener by their neurons of both intellect and passion. Whether oral tradition could ever translate in full measure to the written tradition; whether the passion and richness in masterly writing is the same as in the passion of the spoken word by a great actor: all is a mystery to me. And what of the blind and deaf? Does sign language penetrate to the core like the sounds made by orators, or Braille duplicate the passion of great poetry and if they do not, how can we know this without a viable basis for knowing? Are the deaf and blind limited largely to content and not privileged to the full measure of presentation providing a precious extension beyond content? One thing we do know is the capacity of the available senses to overcome the loss of a sensory member by a heightened awareness developing another pathway to passion. Brain remapping towards communication in fuller measure is truly the stuff of life.

Fleeing from Brain-rot

Pity the poor man at seventy-nine, who wrote of memories galore,
His neural pathways he noted of late, have begun to lose something more.
It's all very well if you're twenty-five, pathways healthy and sound,
Don't take it for granted that they'll survive; hurry to write it all down!

FAMILY

Break-in

The pianist and I were weekending in Lotus Island when we were phoned by the police, who informed us that we had a break-in at our house in Lotus City. The policeman said the house was empty and there was evidence of a ransacking having taken place in the bedroom wing. The security alarm had rung, and the police were prompt to attend, but apparently, whoever it was, had sacked and ran. We had recently established the security system since we wanted to help our daughter feel more comfortable, since she was an older teen and had a life apart from just her parent's cottage. The event was in the days before cell phones and we couldn't get hold of her to check the house for damage, so I just thanked the policeman and said we would call promptly once we were home. The policeman had said that the dresser drawers were all open in a bedroom wing, materials were strewn all over the floor, the clothes cupboard had the drawers all open, clothing and hangers on the floor, the bed and in the hallway. The police response to the alarm was apparently prompt, so the break and enter people probably had little time to search and find, and it was curious that they chose the area that they did. When we arrived back as soon as possible and inspected the bedroom wing where the police had not disturbed the crime scene in any way, it appeared quite normal. The state of our daughter's room was as usual in its distribution of clothing, books and desk materials in an open and readily available state on the bed and floor rather than closeted in drawers. The bed was tousled and slightly made but readied to enter without any effort required to turn anything down other than remove the clothing to the floor. A picture was tilted and the wastebasket was full of paper and peels of orange and banana. Our daughter came home shortly after we arrived and told us she had run out the front door in a hurry and forgot to turn the alarm off and reset it. She said, "I went out so quickly I didn't hear it go off. I'm sorry!" We phoned the policeman and thanked him for his visit. I asked him if he had any teenagers! He said, "No. I'm not married." I told him, "You're in for a treat some day, if you are lucky. In the meantime you can close the case." Love trumps tidy!

The Good, the Bad, the Ugly and the Ridiculous

Like country mice, the pianist and I traveled to Olympic City for the weekend to celebrate my brother's 70th birthday. We were 23 family members gathered there; three generations; and we celebrated in his apartment, high over English Bay with an unimpeded view of the sea, the sunset, the freighters gently anchored out, and the distant and beautiful city lights. It was the Good. Equally high in our city hotel later, we looked down on the flat roofs of adjacent city blocks, covered with moss, green and black, pools of dirty water, spouts and pipes and chimneys and mildewed walls with a tawdry drabness seen from above that is never apparent from the lower levels or the street. It looked like Chim Chim Cheree without the music or dancing. It was the Ugly. From our hotel room in the morning I watched the Dumpster Digger work in what was obviously his lane-way, which was directly opposite my window. He was methodical as he checked his dumpsters up and down the lane every half hour through the morning for the treasures of the garbage. Recycling the throwaway culture in order to eke out a life without hope of finding a beautiful thing. This was the Bad! Across the city from our vantage point on the 19th floor, the adjacent high-rise apartment penthouses displayed rooftop trees, evergreen and deciduous, some as high as 30 feet, guy-wired against the wind. There were forest dwelling penthouse people sighted, strolling around their potted faux forest on the roof! This was the Ridiculous! The love and kindness the three generations of our family felt for one another, of course, transcends all these four images, or goes through them, carrying what is necessary, but in reality needing none of it. That is really the Good that trumped all. Still, we are called upon to look around as we go!

The Hayride

When I was 14 we lived for one winter in Conquest, a small town in Saskatchewan. I played hockey with the town team, which went to Milden, Dinsmore and Outlook in a league of all sorts. Our team was composed of big children and adults, of whom a few were a bit skillful. Those of us without self-transport—the young—accompanied by a few girls, traveled in a truck with a covered box filled with hay and entered by the grain chute at the back. It was cozy and warm and dark with the packed bodies and the smells. There was a sensuality to it all in that era that at 14 we could not identify clearly, but knew there was something stirring about. There was no rolling in the hay in those days, but there was an ill-defined excitement for me from the presence of Lily-Mae, a pretty, lanky, snub-nosed, freckled, longhaired girl that had come to cheer. Just dream on! We were away from the restraints of school and parents and at close quarters. I was still too wrapped-up in myself at that time to have the energy or wherewithal to foster a relationship. My experience of hayrides was finished that spring until I was 21 and met the pianist for the first time on a hayride in Winnipeg. This was a party organized by the student nurses. This time the rack was horse-drawn and it was cold so you bundled up and huddled together to keep warm and tried to hear one another through the din. This leads to a "close for comfort" that casts off the restraint and awkwardness that formality or con-trivance brings. The excitement this time was less ill-defined for me. She was beautiful and fun and I was ready to put some energy into someone other than myself. I don't know what it is about hay, or dark, or cold, or simple pleasures, but I know that the closer you need to be, the closer you will become. There may be something primordial and concupiscent about the influence of hay! Hay is the stuff of legends!

Shit-mix

It may have been the singular moment of awareness when I encountered shit-mix for the first time! Living with three adolescent teen and pre-teen children in Lotus City was a busy time for me and the pianist. Our down time for communication was the supper hour and after that I often went back to work or watched the hockey game. My daughter told me recently that our pediatric set always chose to show me the school report card and get it signed when the game was at a critical spot and before the pianist saw it. They were craftier than I thought! I had remained naively unaware of that subterfuge! She also said that I always told her, "Do better!" without really looking at all the details. I'm not proud of this! Being a parent is always going uphill on a slippery slope. One way to get traction on the slope I finally learned is to combat deception with deception. Also a big mistake. I did learn in time a better way though it took me quite a while. One of my pleasures, aside from hockey, was a varied liquor cupboard with a selection of offerings; another putative parental pitfall! That array provided a welcome choice for an after work libation! I did notice, belatedly however, that my supply was diminishing faster than my efforts could explain, and the leakage was evenly distributed amongst the bottles. The pianist started looking to see how many finger widths were in my glass. I recognized the look, but pled innocent! I began to wise up and, unannounced, marked with a felt pen the existing levels in the bottles. Over the next week or two, most of the bottle contents evenly "evaporated" a half inch! I got a lock for my liquor cupboard door and kept the key. I mentioned to the local grocer, a friend, later in the month that I had solved my problem of the disappearing booze. He said, "The kids from the school are drinking what they call shit-mix! They mix half an inch or so from each liquor bottle and come here for orange crush and put it in their bicycle bottle with the liquor mix! They have a big party at Gyro park! It must taste awful!" I can't say I was surprised. The news was amusing but it just wasn't funny! It was a stunning moment however when I realized that they were flesh! It was like a lock suddenly unsnapped in my head! Time for the family conference. Amazing the good fathering that results when he gets a good kick in the ass and looks in the mirror for the first time. Years later when they all were in their forties we went to Gyro park and sat on the cement octopus and had a beer. We talked about life in the flesh, alcohol swill, kids and shit-mix, but they didn't remember. Maybe they weren't part of the Gyro parties after all, but it was a wakeup call for me then, and a good dollop of Jim-mixing supplanted the bicycle bottle.

Comforting Sounds

As they lie asleep in bed at night with the sound of soft snoring, interposed with episodes of stertorous sounds of air intake from the companion, the gentle dream cries, the rocking noise of the bed from body tossing that are signs of life and provide vaguely apprehended comfort as the listener senses, through the haze of sleep, the continuation of the life force, in place at least for one more night. His old smoker's wheeze from time to time, little groans, words to no one, and the thrash of an arm gives a sense of vitality in the dim room, that another day of togetherness will survive. The coughing and sniffing sounds rising up with the flatfooted beat and huff and puff on the stairs, announces his reconnection, without which loud silence is felt in the void. The sharp echoes of argument and passion defeat the unconnectedness of indifference! There is no soundlessness here which leads to gulf and distance. Passion and laughter give a form of music, both harmonious and dissonant, but that leads to an essential roundedness. Sitting on the medical ward in the still of the night; making hourly rounds; listening carefully to the comforting sounds through the dim light by the bedside, blesses the tiptoe listener with the music of the hospice that soothes. Comforting sounds from the crib with the nightly vigil of the night visitor who leans and rearranges the blanket tossed, and gathers in the sounds as soothing recognition of life, listened for and heard. A still small cry from the depth of rubble, or the fearful possibility of an airless shaft, announces life to the frantic rescuers and comforts someone, somewhere, with sounds that a blessing is possible and what cannot be seen, nor can be touched, is music that sings to each of us. Sounds of life: all are Harmony Divine!

The Familiar

"Look!" I said to the pianist this morning, "There is the flock of American widgeons that has returned. They weren't here yesterday." They are the first returnees of our winter ducks. What is it about the familiar that is so comfortable? Expectations met! The orb is turning as it ought! November is a black month here, but the dark, wind, and cold is familiar, so it is welcome. The widgeons tell us it is good to be here! They say, "This is where we choose; this harbour and you are our familiar. You can rely on us and the buffleheads and the others that return for the winter to soothe your familiars." The older one becomes, the more familiars one has and the more they become of value. My kids, when they were young, liked the same story over and over again. If I changed it a little bit they objected, "That's not right Dad. Tell it the way you're supposed to." They were young, so had developed fewer familiars and what they had was precious to them. Breaking new ground, on the other hand, is crucial for the young: creating familiars for themselves, though they may not know it at the time. Years ago I had a white cable-knit sweater that I really loved. I wore it a lot, and particularly on my boat with my captain's hat and a scarf: it became a joie de vivre! It was my statement! As it was in frequent use it became frayed at the wrists and the waist baggy. It looked a bit like a tent with the bellybutton sometimes showing, elbow yarn thinned, a bit stained in front, and after multiple washings, the pianist chucked it in the bin to discard. I retrieved it and continued to wear it, averse comments notwithstanding! It was a familiar and I still felt a certain jauntiness it imparted despite its disagreeable appearance. After all, I was the author of its decrepitude and I owed it protection. My efforts to prolong the life of my cable-knit were for naught when the pianist had finally had it with washing it, trashing it, and having it repeatedly retrieved. One day, adversely, she washed the algae and mold off the greenhouse floor with my treasure. It was a dirty grey-green! It was like the day my aunt took away my blanket when I was three. Another familiar bit the dust and as in the children's story telling, I needed to break new ground !

Memory and Acuity

My brother Ken, four years younger than me, has a more accurate long-term memory of the events of our youth than I do. Whereas I recall the emotional effect of the events on me in fairly vivid detail, he has greater acuity for the events themselves. I knew enough to know never to argue with him, because he was almost always right. I had remembered, I thought, of an event in 1946 of which I had been told. My uncle Edgie had been a prisoner of war in Stalag 8B for 3 and a half years after the Dieppe raid. I was telling Ken's son that in prison Edgie had wagered a fellow prisoner that he would swallow a dead mouse for a dollar. I was telling Ken about this conversation and he said, "No, you are wrong, the bet was that he would bite the mouse in half for a dollar." He apparently did! Now neither Ken nor I have talked about this for probably 60 years, but his superior acuity in the matter does not take away from my account of the horror I felt in learning of that event and whether it was biting or swallowing is completely beside the point. My memory is only of my feeling of revulsion, and something about a mouse, dead or alive. So far, this little story has nothing elevating or useful to teach, but I have been reading Roger Lundin's book, Emily Dickinson and the Art of Belief. He says, "—for her [Emily] memory meant the recollection of intense experiences or encounters rather than the rituals of general commemoration. It usually involved the revival of a sensory impress." In addition, he says, "She was intrigued only by the memory of what went on within the dwelling of her conscious life." I think that may be the difference between Ken and me. He saw and remembered the details of what went on in life vividly and accurately. My recollection of the same facts that I would have heard about so long ago is completely colored by the recall of the feelings. The acuity is often swept up by the memory of the feelings, which are the more powerful in me and others. In a world today of law, testimony, false memory syndrome, accusation, redemption, recall, regrets, hurt, loss, acuity, and recompense, justice demands that we stick with the reporter rather than the poet.

Fat Elvis

In retrospect, a useful service a parent can offer a boy in his early teens is to accept the fact that the father can be a foil for certain mirthful commentary by the son and his friends. I learned, through some sort of inadvertency in the grapevine, that I was referred to by the diminutive set as Fat Elvis! I had more girth at that time than Elvis, but I think it had more to do with my 60s hair style, rather than my singing voice or my pelvic inclinations. I wasn't particularly dismayed by this description as I recall, since I considered the source. Besides, I also knew how many teachers I had heard of that had mirthful monikers applied which were litmus indicators of whatever perceived shortcomings the youthful entourage considered were worthy of comment. It is important for a son to have the opportunity to rail away at his father with his friends and to share in the joy of their raillery with one another! Even bad press is at least an acknowledgement that you exist and are somehow looming as a presence. Heaven knows there are far worse labels to apply to a parent than that of an aging Elvis. Elvis Presley and I were the same age so the guerrilla action by this pediatric 5th column was in my case pretty benign and the simile, a step up for a simple, plump and tuneless surgeon. At any rate, they would skulk around, claiming the smell was just Patch, shoelaces untied, and nothing done up, and claiming victory for themselves over The Foil. Little did they realize the honour implied, being compared to one of the finest voices and rhythm makers in the world. I won't say I was glad to be called Fat Elvis as it smacked of schoolboy insolence, but as long as it was behind my back, it remained unacknowledged. All this was forty years ago. I have never yet asked him how that name came about. He may have even forgotten about this period. I just celebrated the fact that a little derision, particularly with your friends when bravado is needed, remains part of the important and necessary distancing process! I could have got back at him by calling him "dear" in front of his friends, as I occasionally did when we were alone, but I assiduously avoided this in company. It would have been demeaning at fourteen, but not at forty. Like most conditions in life, if you wait it out in good humour, it also gets better.

Short Pants

I was the last kid in my age group to graduate to long pants. This was a coming of age event for boys in Kindersley, the prairie town where I grew up. That secular coming of age was delayed by my mother's insistence that short pants were less slovenly than long pants, notwithstanding the inevitable dirty knees. Maybe it was easier to insist that I scrub the knees than she wash and iron long pants, but still, short pants weren't any longer cool. I was also the only boy in my age group that had to attend Sunday School and when I finally prevailed upon her to let me absent myself, particularly since at that time my father didn't go to church, I could usefully argue my case. Sunday school wasn't cool either. I was the only boy in the Sunday School other than my young brother and was stuck with horrible girls as well. My young brother didn't count. I argued that since I had agreed to confirmation, I might give Jesus a try one day. I stressed might! It was my anti-religious coming of age! The delay in my coming of age from secular and spiritual bondage, now determined my will for freedom to thrive and grow, or so I believed then. Down deep, I would have grieved if my children became cool too soon in life, so in retrospect I thank God for my mother! Moreover, I had bow-legs, a genetic disorder since the paternal family tree records these parenthetic shaped legs of my forebears, seen in photographs from long ago in swimming costumes with frontal views. Otherwise, the legs were mercifully hidden in long pants, a blessing I had longed for as well. It wasn't fair, I thought; all those old fogies could cover up and I couldn't. As an adult, my friend Bill would look at me in the surgical change room when I was in the buff and say, "Testis in parenthesis!" My brother Ken always grieved that we didn't have legs like the tree trunk legs of Buddy Tinsley. Despite the bow-legs, none of our family, to my knowledge, developed osteoarthritis of the knees since the DNA of the family bow-legs gave rise to bilateral Tibia Vara, so the knee joints were preserved. I think that was lucky. Uncool bow-legs mercifully finally covered up with long pants, and finally baseball Sunday morning, not Sunday School, so lucky in the the coming of age. It took me longer to realize it wasn't me; it was mini-me; it was good then;

it is good now; it was good that my mother was right, and I finally gave lucky Jesus a chance!

An Act of Care

My father came into the bedroom of my brothers and me every night before he went to bed, pulled the covers back up on us and tucked us in. Then, he always got up in the middle of the night to cover us up again. We always had the vague sense that a hand was present and a vigil performed. This act was probably often unnecessary, as our rooms were warm in those latter days, but he was functioning out of a long-standing habit. Our covers were often kicked off because young boys are restless sleepers; at least we were; fidgeting night and day! Where did that routine of his come from? Possibly an automatic act from the need to show us protection through the darkness of the night and its terrors! A form of gathering us in! More likely the act arose from our family moving from cold boarding houses to cold boarding houses regularly every few weeks during the tail end of the great depression in the late '30s and '40s when he worked on the railway spare-board. Probably also however, when we finally got a house and it was cold in the middle of the night when he got up to refuel the coal fired furnace. I don't think, I confess, ever doing that nightly act with my children! It's only now that I think about that act as one of care, a visible sign of an invisible impulse of love. We do little things to signify love! Different things unique to each of us. Different ways of expression! My dad's was one of his unique acts! These acts can only signify what they mean for us, and what they meant to them at times when we reflect on it. Hey! That was an act that I never really recognized the significance of at that time. It was just accepted that it was what he always did even when it was not necessary. The small and seemingly inconsequential visible signs of parental love so often are under the radar until your soft wear revisits and reawakens the feelings of the event, because you inadvertently pressed a little used old keyboard button! When I read Robert Munsch's gentle children's book "Love You Forever", it made me wish I had tucked in the covers more often for my mother and father before they died! It was then that I realized it was a book for big people too.

The Wonders of Wax

In the early '70s the pianist and I, on an impulse to fulfill our role as guides to improving the minds of our children, embarked on family viewing of a programme called The University of the Air. At that time, the television set was in what we called the TV room: a tiny room in which we had inserted soundproofing to the walls so as to avoid the noise pollution disturbing the so-called cultural sanctity of the rest of the house. The programme had been developed by CTV and began at 6 AM for a half hour with a variety of topics, presented largely as lectures. We had been given an electrical warming platter by a grateful patient so the pianist used it to keep our porridge warm as we all assembled at 6 AM in a tight little crowd to watch and listen as the lecturer discussed the Wonders of Wax for the half hour, or other equally dismal topics. This meant, of course, that we awoke at the ungodly hour of 5:30 AM to make breakfast before the programme. In retrospect, to have imposed this unconscionable event on three little children from 9 to 14 years of age, not accounting for the unspeakable drear for the pianist and me as a start to our busy day, was education gone mad, breakfast interruptus, and well-meaning insanity. Thank goodness the grumbling from the pediatric set soon brought an end to this mis-attempt at togetherness and we all went our own way without any further necessity to ruminate on the wonders of wax. I do think, however, given a topic like the wonders of wax, the real wonder is that CTV was able to continue this programme from 1966 to 1983. They probably got a Canada Culture Grant. Our mistake! To err is human, to forgive, divine!

RECREATION

The Story's Butt End

It was often my habit on a work day, to go fishing at daybreak off the waters of Lotus City! I would start at 5 am and finish before 8 am, change on the boat and go to work. I fished alone at that time of day and there was nothing more pleasant than to troll along the Discovery Islands at Strongtide Bay on ebb-tide, with the wire lines humming and the trolling bells on the rods rhythmically ringing with the gentle tug and swell. Because it was early morning, nature usually called sometime shortly after the setup, and in the cabin on the throne I would rest a bit, watching and listening to the bells through the open cabin door, in repose, with an air of contemplation and expectation. The joy I felt on the briny deep in pursuit of the salmon was enhanced by the embrace of Mother Nature, who was mine alone at that time of the morning. The world was still asleep! My lines were fishing deep, the depth maintained by planers, that when tripped by a strike prompted the rods to ring the bell urgently. The planers rose to the surface quickly with the fish on, causing line slack. The fisherman always needed to act with alacrity to get to the rod and tighten the slack to avoid the fish throwing the hook! In the midst of my meditation, suddenly the bell rang stridently on the starboard rod and with great speed I hopped off the throne, pants dangling at the ankle; I bounded to retrieve my rod from the rod holder and began to reel in the slack to tighten the line and start to play the fish! I suddenly heard great cheering and looked up to see high fives from a quartet of tourists on the guide boat, fishing long-side me, starboard. My boat had little freeboard so I wasn't entirely sure that they were cheering my catch or my crotch! I wasn't fishing for compliments but so much for ego! Thank goodness it was a time well before cellphones with cameras and Youtube. You can't hold your rod and wind up your knuckleduster reel and pull up your pants, all at the same time unless you have three hands. Something had to be let go and it wasn't the fish.

The Start and Finish of Golf

During the war years, when we lived on the bald prairie in Kindersley, Saskatchewan, I golfed with my mother. I was from 7 to 10 years old at the time and golfed with her clubs, sharing them as we went around the 9-hole golf club south of the tracks. I don't think the course was ever irrigated: I remember it as always brown with oiled sand greens. The entire course was as flat as a pancake. It even had the occasional cow turd as I recall, so the cow pie rules allowed a change of lie. It was rough where it was trod and really rough where it wasn't! Mum and I both loved fried mushrooms and part of my job while playing was to dig them up as we went around. The best ones were the mushrooms that hadn't yet emerged, but showed the telltale cracking of the dried crust of earth. She and I would have a feast when we got home. My mother was a dreadful golfer, but determined, and a round with her consisted of a swing, an oath, always "damn," and, moving forward, ignoring the divot. I created another divot from my mushroom digging. I stopped golfing after age ten for baseball, until I turned fifty when my friend George said to me, "Warren, If you don't start golfing now you will never be any good." I took it to heart and joined the Lotus City golf club, beautiful links, and the pianist bought me an enormous collection of clubs for my birthday with a bag that was so heavy I could hardly carry it. Many of my friends and colleagues golfed there, so I bought classic clothing in order to look the part, along with golf gloves, umbrella, ball retriever and Gor-Tex rainwear. I dutifully took lessons and practiced all aspects of the short and long game. George was overly-optimistic; I remained as lousy a golfer as my mother despite my best efforts. It wasn't all bad. I never kept score so I could always regale myself about the four great shots I had over the 18 holes. I was an agreeable golf partner, so was sought after by the equally agreeable since I was so bad it made them feel good about their own game. I felt this was a useful service. The only downside of the golf course, recognized as one of the most beautiful in the country, for me, was that there were no mushrooms.

Fishing with Children

I have a photograph of my eldest daughter when she was 9, standing on the dock in Cowichan Bay, holding, with both hands, a 22 pound spring salmon that is two thirds of her height, which she caught while trolling in the bay. In the late fall, if rain was still slight, the rivers were low and the big fish could not go up them to spawn till the rains came. As a result, the big fish accumulated in the bay, stayed bright, and fishing was spectacular. River mouth fishing is no longer allowed there for very good reasons. I have a photograph of my youngest daughter when she was 9, taken near the end of day at the end of the fishing season in Lake of the Woods, when we were due to go back to the coast. She rowed out to the pickerel hole by herself for the last time. She came rowing back to the cottage near dark, in jubilation, having jigged with minnows for 2 hours, carrying a 6-pound pickerel, the largest of that season. I have a photograph of my son when he was 11, whose line we thought hit bottom around Fiddle Reef, off Lotus City waters, and I scolded him for not watching the line carefully enough to avoid snagging. As we dragged and hauled and backed up the boat to pull at different angles to relieve the snag, we pulled in a dead weight, 44-pound halibut. The halibut suddenly became alive on the bottom of the boat once gaffed and landed and it took a time and effort to subdue it since we didn't carry a 22. When I went fishing with my 10 year old grandson at Batt Rock, a submerged mount in Ganges harbour, we illegally tied up to the can buoy that marked it to still fish and he caught an 18 pound silver green ling cod. Unfortunately, ling cod were out of season and he had to throw it back. I wish now we hadn't made him do it. Principle be damned! He wrote of his sorrow. They are now 52, 49, 54 and 24, but those are fish to remember and there is an imprint on the software gyrus of each, labeled Desire, that portends danger for some fish, some where, some time!

Testing by the Waters

You never know what you and your boat are capable of until you are tested by the waters. Some may say a baptism of fire but I say, "a baptism of water," or at least a good whack with a cheap bottle of champagne. Once tested by the waters, one can say, "I know that I can cope with that much storm and get through it, which opens my range of possibilities." When our family fished in a wooden cabin cruiser we had for over twenty years, it was scary at first, running the inland Salish Sea. I had passed the Power Squadron course and read a book on seamanship as well, but I was untested. At first I made tentative forays on calm days till I mustered up courage and took three of my friends for an extended long weekend of fishing several kilometers off shore. The weather was calm for two days and we had a great time putting into moorages along the way and celebrating our feats of seamanship on land and sea. One of the friends warned that there was a weather change coming on the last day, but by then we were cocky about our newfound skill. On the way back to the home port the weather changed and the wooden dingy blew off the transom in the heavy seas and broke up. We watched the pitiful sticks tossed away in the wake. We secured our life jackets, reduced our speed, and stayed white-faced as we silently held our breath at the large following high seas that swung her backside from side to side for hours until we entered the first safe harbour along the way, still far from home. We anchored out and called to the waterfront houses till someone rowed out and rescued us. The pianist picked us up and drove us home. She said to all of us as she opened all the car windows, "You guys really stink." Residual fear and three days in the same underwear. That of course, compounded the chagrin. Sailors indeed. Stinky, sweating, non-sailors indeed. That foolhardy experience, notwithstanding however ill prepared I was, taught me what our old boat could cope with; tested by the waters. Yet, whatever foolhardy lack of preparation was present, I learned in spades. I too was tested by the waters and found wanting far more than my craft was. It's hard to learn everything from a course when fear will teach you from experience. As one prepares for, and ventures forth from what you thought were your limitations in life, as in the limitations of your craft, one can push the boundary further and further incrementally, always aware of the endpoint of pushing the boundaries to foolhardiness. Like your craft, you have to advance only at the rate conditioned by your own hull speed, the boat's hull speed, and the skill acquired in managing it in storms. There has never been a shortage of risks, but calculating risk only comes with experience. Mistakes, if you survive, can frequently teach more than success. Remaining forever in safe harbour, risk averse, teaches little!

Fishing Story

Some years ago, when we as a family often fished off the Lotus City waters, the pianist's aunt and uncle and married children, a farm family, came from South Dakota to Lotus City for the Christmas season. On a beautiful winter's day, several of the party, including the pianist's uncle, went fishing with me to Fiddle Reef. Now Fiddle Reef is aptly named because the reef is the shape of a violin and is marked by a navigational buoy at the wide end, where through traffic is heavy, and at the stem-end by another buoy, where fishing traffic is heavy! The rock is low enough in the water that at maximum low tide it doesn't dry. We all had planned to have supper at the marina after the fishing excursion, so the others gathered at the appropriate time in the evening. I was absolutely intent on my guests catching a fish and trolled for the entire afternoon around the outer margins of Fiddle Reef, delicately avoiding grounding our lures on the reef! They all took turns with the lines, but despite my best effort––nothing! The pianist's uncle was one of those special gentle human beings and it was his turn on the lines. The rest of the family had gathered at the marina restaurant and they could see us at Fiddle Reef, still fishing in the gloom. We were running lights on by then, and it was cold, so we trailed clouds of steam as we went back and forth in terminal desperation to catch a fish. The season was such that these fish were almost entirely winter spring salmon of 5 to 15 pounds, developing size on winter bait at that time of the year. Suddenly, as we were about to give up, a line screeched into action and a fair sized fish started breaking water at a tremendous speed, shaking and writhing with each jump. Fortunately, it was a Penn reel rather than a knuckle duster, so our uncle could play the fish more easily. The violent action at the end of the line did not abate for some time. I ventured to everyone on the boat that it was a large coho because a spring salmon, as I said, rarely, if ever, leaves the water in its struggle to free itself. Was I ever wrong! One thing the spring salmon does to a bait fish ball is to enter the school with its tail lashing, crippling some of the small bait fish, and then turning and eating the crippled fish at leisure. However, sure enough, the 10-pound spring salmon we hooked, was hooked in the tail. It behaved like a coho only because of that. I had never seen a tail-hooked fish before or since, but that seems strange in retrospect because of the manner by which the salmon generally, within a bait fish school, cripples them before it returns to eat. That's why almost all salmon lures are created to simulate crippled bait fish. Salmon, like all of us, prefer getting things the easy way and having a leisurely meal. We got back to the marina to join the crowd who forgave us for the wait. Our uncle had lots of fun fishing, but when he went home to South Dakota he said he had quite a "tale" to tell.

Orca Incident

I often fished in Pedder Bay, near Lotus City, and the most productive area was particularly near the mouth of the bay around the Race Rocks where sea life was abundant and the food chain in full swing. The so-called top of the chain in that area, killer whales, were also abundant! A local entrepreneur in the '70s developed a market for captured killer whales and Pedder Bay was used to create a holding pen for those herded Orcas, to be sold to provide stock for marine shows throughout North America! Since our boat was moored in Pedder Bay for the summer at times, the whale pen was always a point of interest. Several adult whales were confined in a good portion of the bay by submersed netting with surface floats that were well demarcated and the whales could be seen swimming at the surface. My friend Bill, son Robert and I were fishing one beautiful summer day, and I said to Bill, who I thought had not been to Pedder Bay before, "Have you ever seen the whale corral here in the bay?" "No," he said. I told him we would drift close to it so he could take good look. On the way back from our fishing trip, I cut the engine when we were near the pen so we could sit and watch. I was not prepared for how fast the tide was running and since we were without power, the boat slid gracefully over the netting into the centre of the pen. The whales had company. My boat was a displacement hull and the propeller was almost three feet below the water line. I could envision in an instant, ripping out the net with my propeller; creating a big enough rent in the pen to allow several million dollars worth of whales to make their escape. Bill, whose seamanship was of low quality, made his way to the cabin to make a cup of coffee. I don't think the whole truth had yet dawned on him or else he was disavowing us! My 12-year-old son was just excited to be in whale company. The whales seemed, on the other hand, totally indifferent to us. They seemed happy enough. I couldn't chance powering over the net with a running propeller, so I started the boat at one end of the pen and raced to the other side, cutting the power at the last moment and allowing the way to carry me over. Luckily for us, there was both no damage and there were no observers. Release or contain! I strained to hear them say what they wanted! They didn't know me well enough to confide, but they cheered my escape. Pathetic Fallacy? Well, maybe! But I was sure I heard the word "Freedom!"

WORK

Identity, Our Tool is Us

It's fall out today and I cranked up my Bearcat Shredder and munched and ground up my pile of pruned twigs and branches to pulp. I am old and feeble and have Rheumatoid Arthritis but with my tool as an extension of me, I am mighty! I am Marlboro Man at work, employing a machine in a rugged activity that my forefathers, at my age, could have only dreamt about. I eventually ran out of gas at the same time as the Bearcat, so both of us called it a day! We all have tools that can be an extension of our arm or leg or brain or senses that make us explorers, visionaries, artists and rugged adventurers! Whoever said, "It's not important what you do, but who you are" was not telling the whole story. We are creatures of our tools. In the olden days my father would watch my mother cut slices from the bread loaf. She exerted pressure, forcing the knife down heavily onto the loaf, rather than deftly sawing with light downward force. She was always in a hurry. Her bread slices ended up crushed to about an inch high. He would look at us and intone, "Let the tool do the work." Good advice! When the first primate, or the first crow, used the first tool to do a job that they had originally used an arm or beak to do, they began the process of advancing to a new identity that separated one from another. The artistry displayed by the operator of the excavator is astounding, who with foot and hand, working them together in harmonious accuracy, can practically pick up a small pebble, or lift a one ton rock with his bucket. The machine has become a part of the body. With time and skill the tool incorporates into the organism so there is no space in between the two. There is an area on the gyrus for the tool! Whether the golf club, the hockey stick, the brush, the egg whisk, the ivory keys, the strings, the cup, the pottery wheel or the scalpel; when you have arrived at that golden moment when you are one with your tool, you will no longer see yourself apart from it!

Dry Land Farm

In Saskatchewan in 1950, when I was in grade 12, a mandatory course in the provincial curriculum was called Agricultural Economics. It represented more than just another course. It was a signal that reflected the cultural imperative for the bald prairie following the hardships of the dirty thirties and the efforts of the PFRA (Prairie Farm Rehabilitation Administration) to ensure that improvements in dry land farming would never again allow those dreadful times to recur. The shelter belts, contour plowing, deep furrow planting, stubble retention, summer fallow, early maturing wheat and prairie grass seeding were implemented in my time in the forties and fifties and were a deep and abiding part of our prairie culture as evidenced by the curriculum in school. In Kindersley in the '40s I still vividly remember the wet rags around the windows during frequent dust storms, the relentless wind blowing the Russian Thistle across the bald prairie, unhampered by fences, seeding as they tumbled into the piled up top soil in the ditches. Later, in Conquest, the planted 12-foot Carragana hedges (Siberian peashrub) served as shelter belts; planted in rows every eighth of a mile to check the wind erosion and preserve the blowing snow drifts for precious water retention for dry fields; the hedging protecting the roads from excess snow when we went to school by cutter. Many years later I couldn't even imagine such a course in high school that would so reflect overarching cultural mores and direct its interest to everyone of school age to the economic importance of preservation. I have changed my mind. That zeal we felt then has reappeared in new clothing. Dressed in today's energy toward a green revolution, and the ecological drive manifest by today's youth who are addressing a new problem with the same commitment and zeal that we had. Maybe harnessed with the same school effort that we were privy to! I don't have my essay from Grade 12 now, since I haven't saved my paper from 61 years ago, but I remember I got an A+ from Bill Cybulski for my report on the work of the PFRA. The changes were a matter of survival as a prairie society at that time. We knew nothing then about the presence of oil, potash, uranium or diversity of grains. For me, it is wonderful to watch today's economic renaissance in Saskatchewan, coupled with the need to achieve balance with the environmental largess we have been given!

Punching in

In the summer between 3rd and 4th year Medicine, I was living in Olympic City on the North Shore with my parents in order to save more of my money from my summer job. I was working at the Canadian Fishing Company in the frozen fish warehouse as a fish-piler. I had done this job in Prince Rupert the two previous summers. It was 1955 and the first ferry across Burrard Inlet left the foot of Lonsdale at 6:30 AM and docked at the foot of Gore Street at 7:00 AM. I ran one block to the Canfisco Freezer and punched in at 7:04 AM every day, four minutes late for work! The last cheque I got at the end of the summer was docked two hours pay for my unavoidable late punch in. For years I always felt a twinge of irritation at the company for being so cheap. I was the only summer student working there and they had hired me for the halibut rush as I had worked in Rupert before, so was an experienced fish-piler. During the summer the union had threatened a strike and when we voted I was the only one who voted against a strike. I needed to work. I knew the union was irritated with me but they knew my position and weren't mean! I was grateful for their forbearance and support. Then, years later, I had a patient who was a manager of the fishing company branch. I told him my story, thinking he would be embarrassed. He said, "I know about that! It wasn't the company! It was the union. They told us if you were allowed four minutes of grace every day, they insisted each member receive the same or be compensated with two hours extra wages. It was easier and cheaper for us to dock you the two hours. Besides that," he said, "You probably took home at least two hours worth of fish in your lunch bucket that summer." Hand in the cookie jar! He turned the tables on me. Don't start what you can't finish! I relished being a victim of a big corporation in the past, but can no longer trash the virtue of management at the Canadian Fishing Company! I still am sorry about the union, but I didn't realize the bounty I could have provided them if I wasn't docked the pay. No wonder they weren't mean.

A Good Worker

If I heard it once, I heard it a thousand times when I was growing up on the bald prairie! It may have been one of those prairie truisms that arose out of pioneer stock and depression realities. It was a black and white judgment and the criteria for a "good worker" at that time comprised time spent (endurance), muscle (strength), consistency (reliability) and promptitude (on time), rather than cleverness! My dad was my source for these criteria and he had a lot to say about people who were, by his estimate, not good workers, including such as: those with a beard, those who might be glimpsed with their hands in their pockets, and those standing still. Imbued as I was with his mantra, I never wanted to appear as if I wasn't in constant motion, doing something, almost anything as long as there appeared to be action in order to avoid being labeled a bad worker. As an old man, I still have an unreasonable fear to be seen lolling about if a cleaning woman or gardener or tradesperson is here, working for us. I race to get dressed in my work clothes before they arrive, loath to be seen as one of the idle self-indulgent! I have never grown a beard or put my hands in my pockets without immediate withdrawal of something from them: anything! When I first went to England in 1961 with my little family to live and work as an orthopedic registrar, the pianist and I were invited to a large cocktail party by way of initiation to the community; it was a mixed gathering. I inquired, in the usual Canadian manner of starting a polite conversation, to a gentleman I met of about the advanced age of forty, "What do you do?"—"Nothing," he replied, "Mummy left me pots!" He smiled indulgently! Canadian eh! I don't think I have ever heard such a response since, nor had I ever heard it before, given as a simple statement of fact without a scintilla of embarrassment. Coming from a working class prairie environment I found myself in awe of his genuine self-satisfaction that didn't require him to scurry around and appear to be working in order to justify his existence! I don't think I ever have, or will, achieve that sense of comforting entitlement. Still haunted by reward and punishment. Just desserts from the sins of the fathers!

Diurnal Rhythm

If you have to take a nap or siesta after lunch, or struggle to stay awake in the early afternoon; if you wake up in the middle of the night for a period and struggle to go back to sleep; where these episodes are consistent, your circadian rhythm often does not easily blend in for yourself, or for the many employers in today's workaday Western world. Those of us who have two sleep/wake periods rather than one sleep/wake period in the circadian cycle have struggled. Now that I am retired I can embrace my true, modified circadian rhythm. Even though so much is known about the biological nature of the circadian cycles, how they exist throughout all nature and are endogenous, without the ability to fully adapt to externals, we have not effectively implemented change to address the matter. We have not sought where possible to adapt work to the cycles, rather than forcing adaptation of the cycles to the job. As interns working in hospitals, we were often on call and busy 18 to 20 hours at a time. Circadian cycles were completely ignored by those who trained us, since the received wisdom of the time was that it was good grounding for us. It was said to toughen you up for the real world. We had alert periods and less alert periods in the 24 plus cycle. We were less alert during the afternoon for some of us and more alert at one am for some of us. How pathetically ignorant and dangerous it was for patients who were treated by us in the wrong circadian sleep cycle, apart from the length of the on-call time. The interruption of the cycle by nurses working 12-hour night shifts and adapting to turn around to 12-hour day shifts, hard on the heels of one another has the same built-in fault, both in respect to patient care and nurse's general and cardiovascular health. For those nurses with four-part rhythm, it meant working out of cycle, part-time, twice per-24 hours as well as reversing the out of cycle changes every few days. What a burden. Sadly, those who have to manufacture energy, often trumping the natural rhythm of their organism, are stuck with adapting to the external demands of work. A paramoecium embedded in a milieu not of one's own natural order! At least, by acknowledging this concept, one will erase blaming oneself for periodic torpor and give one the hope that retirement will allow the natural man to emerge! The creative thrust in life comes from the alert rather than the weary, both at work or play.

Self Publishing

My experience in self-publishing has been stimulating and exciting, but a financial bust. I would do it again in an instant for the self-gratification it brings and the heartening responses from my family and friends! Writing becomes an intimate relationship with yourself and built into that dual persona are both a speaker and a listener. Why not record the dialogue? If not therapy, at least it is self-examination since all writing is in a sense biography. If you have narcissistic and compulsive tendencies you can build on your useful personality traits and put them to work. The book I previously wrote, "An Elderly Eclectic Gentleman," was taken from a blog over the three-year period and edited for publication by myself. The self-publishing company was helpful throughout the period of production and the cost was not exorbitant. Don't expect the self-publishing people to market it for you. I have some weaknesses, not the least of which is, I don't have the balls to market myself. I am sure my weakness can be attributed more to pride than sense, but I do not wish to go hat in hand to a commercial publisher at my age! Fear of failure maybe; fear of reality possibly; perhaps fear of discovery of the hollow I may carry. Still, I have the perennial optimism that I may be discovered eventually. My previous book is 294 short topics on the real and mystical world around us that I have encountered. If I went to a commercial publisher I figured they would delete a third of my work for market reasons and I didn't want my muse assaulted and my therapy insulted. Besides, the real me has always been a composite of well-done and badly-done. Therefore, I am poised, willingly, to put my ass on the horns of my own dilemma. So be it! In the meanwhile I continue to write because I can't avoid writing from time to time when the impulse occurs. My theme is the ordinary is almost always extraordinary in some settings and life is a mystery. God is a mystery to me as well, but there always seems such an Immensity in much of life that is both constant, yet evanescent. Maybe that's it! It's hard to get around the cognitive dissonance that ordinary is extraordinary, and constant is evanescent when one attempts to replace sex, violence and cynicism with wonder! Well, what the hell: record it anyway!

SYMBOLS

Magpie Man

When I consider collectors, (me, the magpie, and the dog), the dog and the bird have a different character and I find myself in between them in the spectrum of the collectors. I collect ugly but functional junk to lighten the workload; the magpie, shiny junk to seduce his lady; the dog, however, buries its junk, food, and spit slippery toys to avoid sharing until the food turns and becomes more tasty and the toys dry out! The magpies are more like the glitterati than the dog and me, and a lot meaner. In point of fact, there looms in each of us that demon: pride. I, for example, am cheap, and cut up some old leaking hoses that others would chuck, to thread old wire through the cut segments, to secure for instance a heavy Wisteria to the eaves or brace small trees. The hose segments do not cut or traumatize the branches in the wind and also shed the damp rapidly. My breast beats away with pleasure at myself for my inventiveness and frugality. An unalterable penchant for neatness and order from some will result in a loss of valuable materials to a dumpster that the more frugal will readily apprehend as worthy. This wastefulness permits me the joy of some scorn. On the other hand, the male magpie is a notable collector of junk, particularly the shiny, or colour-ful. The magpie's junk is kept close at hand to the nest area, easily accessible and even rotated when boredom with his toys begins, or if inattention of his mate mandates a change! His display is important. Unlike the magpie, I maintain my tawdry junk invisible, but it is still near my nest where it is instantly accessible. Out of sight, but not out of mind applies with me, because I know storage and dead storage is dynamite to find things in unless a distinct written inventory is at hand. The difference with the Magpie is his shiny stuff is all for show and not for blow and since he can't write an inventory, he needs to keep it out on display where he doesn't forget, and where the lady magpie needs to see evidence of his continuing manly interest in her and trinketry. On the further other hand, most dogs are also collectors, but unlike the Magpie, their treasures are all functional. Food or toys! Toys mercilessly chewed! Many dogs do not squirrel these two away underground, but there is always a subset of collector dogs. That dog always buries a bone or excess bread heels or his toy and will not always remember the whereabouts of these treasures despite the best of noses, unless he takes a leak on the soil to mark it. Neither the magpie nor I have that inclination. I find myself situated in between the magpie and the dog, as between secretive and miserly like the dog in the manger, and approaching proud and possessive like the magpie. All of us hubristic: arrogant in glitter and equally arrogant in parsimony!

The Unsung

The crawl space of the house on Lotus Island that belongs to the pianist and me is three feet high, large and labyrinthine in nature. When traversing the labyrinth on one's belly and knees, the pink insulation that hangs down loose from aged split bindings, spookily brushes one's face in the dark while undulating, crawling, wiggling body movement causes cement dust to stir up little storm clouds, and we sense the sounds of fluids running in and out the many pipes, ingressing and egressing to and from the house, giving one's hand a little thrill as the myriad of pipes softly vibrate in response to the flow. Here is a world alive; apart but connected to a house above that credits little to its dependence on the vital and visceral nature emanating from this dark region. There is no area so underestimated in importance as this subterranean world. The heat, the light, the water, the ventilation, the septic system, the Internet, the communication, all arise from Action Central, the crawl space. I like being there because one is right at the source, the vital organs, where every thing else hangs in its balance and there is a deep understanding provided of the house's kinetics. It is the place where they all begin, and where they all draw from, and connect to the world around. The umbilical cords of the house from the placental world. And yet, the realtors never sing the praises of the crawl space. The purchasers never celebrate the crawl space with its firm and anchoring foundation walls. No poet creates a panegyric to this footprint of the house that serves so well, yet is unsung. Some of those with a more delicate nature may find it arduous and unpleasant to enter this dark world on their belly where the possibility of vermin and wasps and bees and ants may coexist. These dark-adapted inhabitants won't adversely affect Action Central. They just know a good place when they find one. Our exploration, like an exploratory laparotomy, marvels at the beauty of the vital organs in action. My son-in-law and I just spent an hour in the crawl space, worming our way through the labyrinthine apertures to all the low hanging rooms of this underworld; celebrating each by prostrating ourselves to the wondrous foundations, the wires and pipes and cables and in prostration, received the emanations of the house where it counts; from the bottom up.

Force Vitale

My architect friend, who designed and supervised the building of a house for the pianist and me in 1970, phoned yesterday to tell me it was featured at a 3-month Legacy Show in a gallery in Lotus City! The house, though only 38 years old, had also been designated earlier, by the Municipality of Saanich, as a heritage house. The house broke new ground at the time in the seventies, though in retrospect, it certainly wouldn't have been everyone's cup of tea. I had friends that felt sorry for us, others that said it looked like a bank, but we ignored them since we had by then, crossed the Rubicon. Still, it was interesting and exotic and after it was built the architect told me that he was most appreciative of the fact that he had a free hand throughout the design and building process; a situation he rarely encountered. The pianist and I were young, and I, at least certainly felt at the time sufficiently naïve that I had no right to tell someone as knowledge-able as an architect what he should build. We came and watched it being built and growing every day and it became slowly our own so when we moved into it, we adapted and the house became our home and we knew every stick. A house is only a home when a heart beats strongly within it! Mine did, and so did my sense that I had somehow arrived when the erotic house seductively took up my identity within itself. We sold the house after seventeen years when our needs changed, but I never forgot the house throughout the intervening years, as it was my statement throughout the time we lived there! When we left and the furnish-ings were gone, I never returned to see it because, for me, a part had been excised. The pianist, however, went back to look at the empty house and as she looked in every room she knew: "A house without a force vitale, is only a beautiful empty shell." The heart in any house, whether beautiful or homely, is what creates the home. The pianist shared my feelings about leaving it, but it became apparent to her as she toured the empty house that it was a corpse, albeit a beautiful corpse, without a heart, awaiting a new transplant. I wish now that I had the pianist's foresight to revisit it once it was empty so that I could also write finis to the sense of loss that I felt at that time. The loss of course is never to you, but to the house, since the force vitale is a force the house can never retain, and that we carry with us. I guess we always should assess the relationships we create with our symbols. There is a danger lurking that as times change, the visible symbol as a sign of an invisible presence can become an invisible symbol indivisible from oneself. One needs vigilance to maintain control of one's own orbit.

Battling over Symbols

Logo; a symbol, or sign, that derives from the Greek "logos", meaning word, can be seen to simply represent at a glance what ever it purports to represent. Today we have thousands of logos as symbols but they often have been so graphically reduced that they no longer resemble the image of their original source, and yet once established, the symbol, as a logo, is often recognized, despite the disconnect with its source. The symbol identifies the product, idea, company, profession or activity. The Wand of Hermes, also called the Caduceus, was a stand-alone symbol that once, for a time, was the logo for the medical profession in the United States. The wand consists of a staff with two serpents rampant. It is pretty. The Olympian God, Hermes, or his Latin equivalent, Mercury, was the God of Commerce. Like all Greek gods, Hermes had a variety of other minor related jobs unfortunately, like protecting travelers, including bandits, card players, messengers and any and all on the road. Generally meeting the needs of hustle-bustle but an unfortunate choice for a logo of medicine and eventually jettisoned. However, the Rod of Asklepios is the historically correct symbol of the medical profession and is employed world wide now. Asklepios was the Greek God of Medicine in the Golden Age of Greece, but his Rod, as originally portrayed in tradition, is very ugly. As a stand-alone symbol, the Rod of Asklepios, from the original images, would look like a fat club with a serpent wrapped around it. From all the Greek images it looks like something that would be carried by Alley Oop. It's a saw-off then. The American Medical Association mistakenly at one time, went for the Caduceus, the Wand of Hermes, pretty but inaccurate as an idealized representative of physicians; they unwittingly enlisting Hermes, God of Commerce, and also, Fast Eddy, itinerant travelers, card sharks, banditry, and sharp practice. Canadian physicians, perhaps more aware of Greek mythology, though I doubt it, excised Asklepios from the symbolic image, and tarted up the Rod. Now the designers have reduced the logo of both to cryptic, divorced forever from their origin. The Canadian Medical Association logo is now designed with a straight line and a squigle twisted around it. The

American Medical Association logo adopted the Rod and morphed it now into a straight line with a coil spring around it. Whether it is better to portray the serpent with a squigle or a coil spring is moot. They both agreed with a stroke line for a club. The logo has gone from pretty or ugly to arcane abstractions. If symbolism is a visible manifestation of an invisible ideal, we both chose to symbolize that medicine, in its best cloth, is widely separated from commerce but who, even most physicians, would know that from the logos? That often however may be more of a false hope anyway. In this day and age perhaps we may all want to be pretty and rich, never ugly and never sharp. Truth to tell; there is truth to tell; despite the fine logos, Hermes is still at the door!

The Road

I bought a print the other day of the Camino, the road from France to the Spanish town of Santiago de Compostela. It was in an exhibition series of paintings in our library exploring the nature of roads. Standing on the road; a trail really; was a solitary lengthened shadow of a pilgrim with a stick: the low sun, the sense of impending twilight; and the antiqued paper giving the print of the road a quality of roughness and endless distance. A road always suggests a journey: leaving somewhere, or something, or someone, and going to something, or somewhere. But the gist of the journey is the process, not the beginning or the end. The shadow on the road is fully in contact with it, not just the soles of one's feet, and the shadow looks forward and backward throughout the journey, leading and following, and foreshortened watches the traveler from one side or the other as well, through much of the day. Though the traveler passes through the country, the road, hard and rough, the traveler footsore, he is confined by the direction of the roadway if he is to progress to the intended target. If it's the road to Zanzibar Dorothy Lamour makes with her friends, or the Yellow Brick Road, or the Camino road, the place to be is the place between. This is where we walk a step at a time. In my print, the solitary figure expressed by shadow gives a feeling to the viewer of the loneliness of the roadway. There is no Bing Crosby or Bob Hope to accompany Dorothy! There is no Toto to accompany the other Dorothy! But of course, these are only fantasies of reality on the roadway. There is no bicycle, no automobile, just a narrow road in my print for which each step is the only present and the only reality. My print could have been anywhere because road is a metaphor for life. I have never taken the road to Santiago de Compostela, marking the way to the Cathedral of St. James, and I am too old now to do it, but a road is a road is a road and we all are on a roadway to somewhere and leaving somewhere. It's the process that we live with from that road we decided to take, rather than the goal that will take us somewhere else. How many times did you start with a goal and find during the journey that the real purpose was somewhere else?

NOW

Now the play is over
Now the course is run
Now the clapping's over
What is it we've done?

Printed in Canada